Groupwork
Practice

Tom Douglas

International Universities Press, Inc.
New York

HV
45
.D68
1976 b

Contents

Preface

This book has been written in an attempt to present basic
information for people who are interested in working with others
in groups. The only real justification for including any given idea
or piece of information in this text has been its practical proven
usefulness to the author.

There is a great deal of experimental material about groups
which is available for those with time to read; there is also a
considerable amount of literature devoted to approaches to
working with groups developed by people with sincere intent and
much labour. But the purity of the theoretical approach, while
perhaps providing welcome guidelines through the maze of
complexities which comprises group interaction, probably
achieves success at the cost of limiting perception.

No particular theoretical approach is stressed in this book at
the expense of others, but true eclecticism prevails. The approach
is this: if it works, use it; if it sounds good but doesn't work,
discard it until such time as it may be of value.

Admittedly this mitigates against presenting a coherent theory
of groupwork practice, but to the best of my knowledge no one
has yet successfully completed this task though many have tried.
What evolves from an eclectic approach may well be described as
a set of very practical techniques, methods, or instruments which
are characterized by the use of openness and honesty on the part
of the practitioner.

The book is divided into two parts, each with a basic aim.
Part 1 is concerned with the basic assumptions upon which the
practice of groupwork is founded. The wide theoretical background of group processes is discussed within it, and the problems
of using research material to augment and feed one's practical
knowledge are a major topic. The problem of defining a word as
commonly used as 'group', for it to have any practical meaning, is
discussed. Part 1 ends with a clear statement of which 'basic'
assumptions may really be considered to be basic.

In Part 11 I am concerned to provide information about

groupwork practice, that is, to discuss the starting, running, and ending of groups; the preparation which is so important and those particular, common difficulties with which all group practitioners have to deal and which can be so threatening and so destructive.

Perhaps the most important skill that the group practitioner can acquire is the ability to observe. Our culture tends to condition us to avoid looking at people, with the result that we do not really see what is taking place under our noses. We make people into 'things' because we do not concern ourselves with the person that exists behind the facade. It is axiomatic that prejudice adheres to stereotypes and that close contact with a stereotype tends to reveal the common humanity which was previously hidden.

In a very real sense then, this book is directed at those who are concerned with 'people' rather than things, and the basic philosophy which lies behind it is 'people'-oriented.

Nothing can create a good group practitioner better than guided practice, where the development of skill, insight, understanding, and awareness can grow with some sense of security and support. Unfortunately this is not always readily available and the change from ideas to action based upon those ideas has most often to be made with little or no help. It can be a daunting process. Sensitivity to the needs of others needs to be allied to an awareness of one's own needs and anxieties and how they appear to others and how they affect one's own perception and skill.

Burns expressed it clearly:

Oh, wad some power the giftie gie us
To see oursel's as others see us!
It wad frae monie a blunder free us
                 And foolish notion:
What airs in dress an' gait wad lea'e us,
                 And e'en Devotion!

The 'power' referred to here can only be gained by the constant interaction of an open questing mind with the ideas, attitudes, beliefs, and behaviour of others.

Acknowledgements

Parts of this book have previously been published in other places. The following individuals and bodies are thanked for permission to reprint.

The NTL Institute in respect of 'How to Diagnose Group Problems' by L.P. Bradford, D. Stock, and M. Morwitz in *Sensitivity Training and the Laboratory Approach: Readings About Concepts and Applications* (Itasca, Illinois: F.E. Peacock, 1970). Plenum Publishing Corp.: 'Three Dimensions of Member Satisfaction in Small Groups', by R. Heslin and D. Dunphy, *Human Relations* 19 (1964): 99-112. Association of Psychiatric Social Workers: 'Starting an Adolescent Group: Some Anxieties and Solutions', by H. Gee and P. Kemp, *British Journal of Psychiatric Social Work* 10 (1) (1969): 12-16. A.E. Leach and J. Henderson: 'The "Thursday Club" — An Experiment in Social Group Work', *Social Work Today* 1 (12) (1971): 21.4.

The diagram on p. 141 (*Table 7*) is reprinted from page 139 of *The Small Group* by Michael S. Olmstead, with permission of the publishers, Random House, Inc., © Random House, 1959. Diagram on p. 151 (*Figure 8*) is reprinted from pages 8 and 11 of *Handbook of Small Group Research* by A.P. Hare, with permission of the publishers, Macmillan Publishing Co., Inc., © The Free Press, 1962. The diagram on p. 153 (*Figure 9*) is reprinted from page 72 of *Dynamics of Interpersonal Behaviour* by A. Zaleznik and D. Moment (1964) with the permission of the publishers, John Wiley & Sons, Inc.

The basic assumptions of groupwork

Problems and definitions

A great interest in group phenomena has developed over the last thirty to forty years and psychologists and others have produced a flood of experimental data about groups and the behaviour of group members. In February 1959, A.P. Hare declared that he had discovered 1385 references to small groups and he estimated that they were accumulating at the rate of approximately 200 each year, which, given no proportional increase, would produce in excess of 4500 by 1975.

With this announcement of coverage, all the information required by the clinician and the group practitioner should be readily available, but unfortunately there are problems about this.

The basis of group practice must be knowledge of the way in which groups function; but where is such knowledge to be obtained?

'Ask a group Therapist, a Trainer, or a Teacher what use he could make of the voluminous out-pouring of empirical research on small groups. The unhappy fact is that many, if not most, of the potential consumers of such work feel that such research is constantly asking the wrong questions in the wrong ways and that it is at best irrelevant and at worst inaccurate and misleading.'

Thus Richard Mann (1967), in the introduction to his book, pinpoints the dilemma which exists between small group research and group practice. The problem is ancient and universal, that of the relationship between the theorist and the practitioner, between the researcher and the clinician. In the small group world this relationship has another dimension, namely that of the 'natural' and the 'created' group.

Natural groups, those occurring in ordinary 'life' situations, are notoriously difficult to study because of the difficulties of comparison with controls to ensure that the variables measured are held constant. Researchers preferring the safety of laboratory conditions have 'created' groups for the express purpose of measuring isolated variables. What relationship have the findings made in such circumstances to the groups formed by social workers, therapists, teachers, and others? What seems to be needed is practical information about the way groups function; about the effects various factors can have on the performance of a group; how these factors can be used constructively to achieve certain goals; how individuals interact in group situations, etc.

So great is the interest in using group methods in understanding group processes and functions that it becomes paramount that such information should be readily available. The alternative is that interested people will turn to getting experience in a practical setting with little or no help or guidance, and many unnecessary mistakes and many avoidable hurts will be committed.

The writing of those working with groups has all the defects of clinical work in general, namely of isolated experience, uniqueness and lack of comparability with other similar work in order to elicit common factors. The position is therefore that there is a plethora of research data on small groups, most of which is of little value to the practitioner, and a somewhat smaller amount of writing and comment by group workers themselves which is largely unstructured, repetitive and unrelated, so that accounts of isolated experience form the major part of this material.

Practice inevitably outstrips theory - people faced with a practical problem have a way of attempting solutions, which are only tenuously connected to theoretical knowledge, in order to cope with the pressures of the moment. If these empirical measures are satisfactory, then they become part of the practice knowledge of the people who use them.

The problems then may be summarized as follows:

1. Most of the research material on groups is of no immediate value to the group worker

2. What is of value needs to be translated from theoretical conceptions to action possibilities

3. Other sources of information, i.e. the recorded experience of group workers, is unsystematic and tends to be concerned with isolated experience and needs to be related to the theoretical knowledge

The aim here is to explore a series of topics about group work which seem basic to the performance of it as a practical skill and to present some illustrations which can throw light upon them. In this way, it is hoped to produce a guide for group workers which can be used as a reference for information about the more common problems of practice.

To start this process it is necessary to ensure a common understanding of the basic concept of a 'group' in order to facilitate communication. Definitions in the field of social behaviour are notoriously treacherous, but some semantic basis for discussion is very necessary:

'There are then in sum, five characteristics which distinguish the group from a collection of individuals. The members of the group are in interaction with one another. They share a common goal and set of norms, which give direction and limits to their activity. They also develop a set of roles and a network of interpersonal attraction, which serve to differentiate them from other groups.' (A.P. Hare, 1962)

Much verbal effort has been expended upon defining the word 'group'. As a consequence of this there is much confusion in the literature on the subject and some misgivings about whether everybody is talking about the same entity and thus whether research into the behaviour of particular kinds of groups can, or should be, taken to be relevant to all groups.

The word 'group' is used in everyday life to indicate a number of objects, animals, or ideas, or individuals existing in a given moment of time in a close spatial relationship to one another. Thus the Concise Oxford Dictionary defines a group as
' . . . a number of persons or things standing near together, knot,

cluster, number of persons or things standing near together'. It goes on to indicate that the verb 'to group' means 'form into a group, place in a group *with*; form into well-arranged and harmonious whole; classify'.

The whole basis of this fundamental concept of a group lies solely in a plurality of objects and persons existing in close physical proximity at a given moment in time. Thus, by definition, a rush-hour crowd emerging from the tube-station is as much a group as a football team. Of course this is true, but obviously there are glaring differences between the two examples. People in a crowd must be aware that they are surrounded by other people and may even be conscious of a common purpose - to get home. But they are much more likely to see the others as frustrating obstructions and individuals bent on achieving their own immediate purpose, than as the whole crowd attempting to do something together.

On the other hand, the football team will have learned to operate together in order to achieve their ambitions. They will be conscious of their identity as a team and know that it remains fairly constant. Certainly individual and highly personal ambition will still be there, but the team members will tend to perceive that it will be accomplished through the medium of the team. In fact, if they do not so perceive the possibility of achieving their personal goals, they will tend to look for other possible avenues for achieving them and the team will start to disintegrate.

It is not reasonable to assume that the study of groups can ever be concerned with groups that are transient collectivities. First, such study would be highly impracticable; the group would not stay together long enough for any detailed study to be made. Second, questions of size would be paramount. Where does a group like the rush-hour crowd start and where does it stop? How many thousands of people might it not contain? For a variety of reasons most investigators have turned their attentions to groups that are less transient than a rush-hour crowd. Nevertheless, the problems of investigation which are so crippling in transient collectivities remain to some extent in more permanent groups. Thus some definitions of a group are concerned primarily with size, some with purpose, and yet others with the character of the interaction, and yet others with several factors at once.

Definition

The fact that grouping is a natural phenomenon adds further complications. In human society individuals are in every sense of the word interdependent and group together for a variety of purposes. From this stems a rather tenuous distinction made by some writers between 'naturally occurring' groups like the family, and 'created' groups like the work team. That such a distinction can be seen to exist is without doubt; whether it is strictly relevant to any analysis of group behaviour is another matter entirely.

One of the most frequently used subdivisions of the genus 'group' is called the 'small group', which has the advantage of confining attention to groups with a limited number of members. Cooley is credited with coining the phrase 'primary group', by which he meant groups 'characterised by intimate face-to-face association and co-operation. They are primary in several senses, but chiefly in that they are fundamental in forming the social nature and ideas of the individual' (1929: 23-31).

Shils (one of the people who criticized Cooley's formulation for not being specific enough), together with his colleagues, Parsons and Olds, was concerned with the boundaries of a group (1951). He maintained that members of a group were aware of their membership as a boundary which distinguished them from other groups. Thus E.J. Thomas, after arguing for research to establish a continuum of collectivities, gives the following definition as convenient. The small group, he says, is 'a collection of individuals who are interdependent with one another and who share some conception of being a unit distinguishable from other collections of individuals'.

From the awareness of being a unit some definitions turn to the kind of relationship which exists between the members as a basis of distinction. Thus Freud defined a group as 'a number of indivuduals who have substituted one and the same object for their ego ideal and have consequently identified themselves with one another in their ego' (Brown, 1961: 122). Brown likens the relationship between group members to the relationships between siblings. Other writers like Homans (1950) and Sprott (1970) see the degree of interaction between members as being the fundamental distinction between a group and a collectivity.

Thus, the members interact more with each other than they do with others who are, therefore, non-members.

Golembiewski, discussing the plethora of definitions, discerns what he calls 'designation' of small groups (1962). He postulates three definitions. A small group:

1) consists of a small number of individuals in more or less interdependent status and role relations, and has an indigenous set of values or norms which regulates the behaviour of members, at least in matters of concern to the group;

2) is 'any number of persons engaged in a single face-to-face meeting or series of meetings in which each member receives some impression of the other as a distinct person, even though it was only to recall that the other was present.' (Bales, 1950);

3) is any collectivity.

As these definitions were derived from studies on small groups it must be evident that researchers have a fairly wide field open to them which can still be classified as the 'small group'. From the point of view of the person attempting to understand what is known about small groups, this situation can prove to be both discouraging and disconcerting. Several attempts have been made to analyse small group research to extract and correlate the material, e.g. Hare (1962); McGrath and Altman (1966). Neither of these excellent works concerns itself with what definitions the researchers have given to the groups they analysed. The results thus correlated are drawn from all sorts of groups: from those brought into existence for the sole purpose of experiment to naturally occurring groups; from groups of two or three people to large collectivities; from groups whose existence in time is minimal to groups that have been in existence for years, and so on.

This does not necessarily indicate that such data are invalidated, far from it, but it does offer caution to those who would accept the correlations between the studies as being extremely accurate. It must be true to some extent that behaviour in small groups bears a definite relationship to behaviour in large groups, but there is little evidence to show the nature of this relationship except in the studies of subgroup formation which is really the study of small groups in a particular circumstance. What is more positively true is that the relationships within a group change over a period of time and that there are some indications of the way in which these changes take place. Most experimental groups are formed for the purpose of the experiment and cease to exist when the experimental purpose has been accomplished. They are therefore all groups whose performance is affected by their early developmental stage.

These difficulties are neatly summed up by Golembiewski: while talking about using the word 'group' to cover any collectivity of any size and to relate such disparities together as though they were variants of the same entity, he says 'The underlying and convenient assumptions are, of course, that all human aggregates are groups and that although groups may differ in accidents such as size and research utility, they are not essentially different'. Golembiewski asserts clearly that the available evidence 'does not permit such a liberty' (1962: 34-45).

In this brief discussion of the definition of groups no real attempt has been made to show the infinite variety of definitions which are extant. The main purpose has been to indicate some of the snags which have arisen and will continue to arise from the unproven assumptions that all groups are necessarily the same animal. They may be, and clearly are, related, but the degree of consanguinity has not yet been truly established.

REFERENCES

Bales, R. F. (1950) *Interaction Process Analysis.* Reading, Mass.: Addison Wesley.

Brown, J.A.C. (1961) *Freud and the PostFreudians.* London: Pelican.

Cooley, C.H. (1929) *Social Organizations.* N.Y.: Chas. Scribner.

Golembiewski, R.T. (1962) *The Small Group.* Chicago: Chicago University Press.

Hare, A.P. (1962) *Handbook of Small Group Research.* N.Y.: Free Press.

Homans, G.C. (1950) *The Human Group.* N.Y.: Harcourt Brace.

Mann, R.D. (1967) *Interpersonal Styles and Group Development.* N.Y.: John Wiley.

McGrath, J.E. and Altman, I. (1966). *Small Group Research: A Synthesis and Critique of the Field.* N.Y.: Holt, Rinehart and Winston.

Shils, E.A., Parsons, T. and Olds, J. (1951). Values, Motives and Systems of Action. In T. Parsons and E.A. Shils (eds.) *Towards a General Theory of Action* Cambridge, Mass.: Harvard University Press.
Sprott, W.J.H. (1970) *Human Groups.* Harmondsworth: Penguin.
Thomas, E.J. (1967) Themes in Small Group Theory. In E. J. Thomas (ed.) *Behavioural Science for Social Workers* N.Y.: Free Press.

2

Orientations and basic assumptions

The majority of human groups are established for a purpose.
Sometimes there is more than one purpose and people frequently
join groups to achieve purposes other than those which are
officially recognized as the aims of the group, as for instance
when people join a drama group not so much because of any
dramatic interest they may have, but because of the social
activities such a group would be able to offer.

This being so, the basic assumption is that the groups
established for a given purpose will attempt to achieve this
purpose by employing their members to the best possible use.
Again this is not entirely true, for some groups do not and
cannot employ their members efficiently for a variety of
reasons. Nevertheless, it is true that groups attempt to achieve
their aims by members working more or less co-operatively
together, all having some degree of insight into the purpose for
which they are working.

So far then it is accepted that the group attempts to achieve
its goals through the interaction of its members. Obviously there
are many factors that can influence the interaction of the
members of a group: whether they like one another, how much
say they fell they have in the direction the group as a whole is
going, the amount of resources available, and so on. It would be

expected that a group who dislike one another would tend to perform less effectively in jobs requiring co-operative behaviour than a group whose members were on very friendly terms.

It is these factors which influence, or can influence, the interaction of the members of a group which forms the major part of the subject matter of group dynamics. Unfortunately, the apparent simplicity of this scheme is deceptive because the influence of any factor is not a simple once and for all intervention, nor is the influence applied solely in one direction. Thus, if we say that some of the main factors influencing the efforts of the members of a group to achieve their goal are the qualities of the members themselves, this is fairly obvious. If the group is a tug-o-war team their physical characteristics of tenacity and other personal factors will be very important in whether they achieve their goals or not.

But whether they have been beaten regularly lately, the reputation of their opponents, the amount of support they have got, and many other factors will also tend to affect the result of any competition. Thus, the nature of the task they set out to achieve influences their feelings about the amount of success they may achieve and so the way in which they will tackle it.

Most of the factors which influence member interaction also influence one another. This makes a clear analysis of the effect of some factors rather difficult to come by, though McGrath and Altman (1966) have attempted to indicate the correlations between some of these factors.

Group dynamics is concerned with different ways of looking at groups, that is, ways in which a static analysis of a group can be made. A group in action is rather like a film, that is, the relationships, the action, the positions of members are constantly changing within definite limits. The group is a 'dynamic' activity. A structural analysis is rather like a 'still' shot, which freezes the action, and according to its speed, focus, colour, etc., it offers the possibility of a detailed analysis of a given situation at the time at which it was taken.

Again, this is oversimplified and to this extent untrue. A structural analysis, for instance, of the power relationships within a group made at any given point in time would certainly show a static pattern of relationships, but others taken later would reveal that some of that pattern was in the process of change, also that some of it was inherently stable. It is the latter stable part that permits investigators to talk about 'structure' at all, for it is on the stability of most of the relationships that changes can take place. Without some element of order, all would be in a state of flux and chaos would ensue.

To sum up, group dynamics is concerned with the way in which groups function. It is assumed that the tasks or goals which groups set themselves are a legitimate area of study. The ways in which groups attempt to achieve such goals by the interaction of their members is regarded as a major field of study, as are the factors that influence member interaction. Lastly, the ways in which certain systems within a group can be traced to indicate some of the structural properties of the group are also part of the subject matter.

Figure 1: *A Chart of Group Dynamics*

GROUP GOAL

INTERACTION OF MEMBERS

Qualities of members
characteristics, abilities
personalities, motivations,
position in group

Qualities of the group
cohesiveness, values,
size, communication,
performance, composition
duration, internal structure

Qualities of the task
kind of task, stress,
criteria for completion,
rules, sanctions, and
consequences

Quality of relationships
with other groups and
the community

Psychological structure
Power relations, sociometric
choice, roles, norms, and
group attractiveness

A simple diagram of this orientation can be found above (Fig. 1.). In this diagram the factors which influence member interaction are arranged in four large areas:
1) the qualities of members
2) the qualities of the group
3) the qualities of the task
4) the qualities of external relationships

The fifth large area, psychological structure, which is linked with the previous four indicates the more generally used systems in analysing the structure of a group.

The table below shows some, but by no means all of the simpler links between theory and the variables influencing interaction. It is based upon the assumption that the most essential fact about groups is that they exist for a purpose. This is an assumption which is not universally accepted.

Table 1: Basic Orientation Chart

Theoretical Orientations	*Structure Analysis of Variables*	*Variables which influence interaction*
Field Theory	Group Attractiveness	The Qualities of the Group
Interaction Theory	Interation of	Group Goal(s)
Systems Theory	Role Dynamics	The Qualities of the Task
Sociometric Theory	Sociometric Choice	
Psychoanalytic Theory General Psychology	Norms	The Qualities of Members
Empiricist Statistical Theory		External Relationships
Formal Model Theory	Power Relationships	

Explanatory Note on Chart

Column one *Theoretical Orientations* is taken from D. Cartwright and A. Zander *Group Dynamics* (1953: 26-3):

Column two *Structure Analysis of Variables* shows how the theoretical orientations gave rise to structural concepts e.g. role, norms, etc. Finally column three *Variables which influence Interaction* relates the structural concepts to those definable factors which influence the interaction of members and thus the goal achievement of the group.

Most of the psychological theories of human behaviour which have led to some of the most interesting practical approaches, e.g. Gestalt psychology and learning theory, are subsumed under the *General Psychology Orientation* heading in column one, showing as a direct influence on individuals, i.e. members.

A List of Orientations

1. Field theory. This is the name given to the theoretical approach originated by Lewin (1951). It derives this name from its basic thesis that behavior is the product of a field of interdependent determinants (known as life space or social space). The structural properties of this field are represented by concepts from topology and set theory, and the dynamic properties by means of concepts of psychological and social forces. For an overview of this approach reference may be made to articles by Cartwright (1959a and b) and Deutsch (1954).

2. Interaction theory. As developed especially by Bales (see 1950, ch.30), Homans (1950) and Whyte (1951), this conceives of a group as a system of interacting individuals. The basic concepts of this approach are activity, interaction and sentiment, and the attempt is made to construct all higher order concepts from these terms.

3. *Systems theory.* The view that a group is a system, adopted by the interaction theorists is also found in a wide variety of forms in other writings. These may be referred to as systems theories. Thus 'systems of orientation' and 'systems of interlocking positions and roles' are central conceptions in the work stimulated by Newcomb (1950); the notion of 'communication system' has been widely employed in research following the leads of communication engineering; and the conception of a group as an 'open system', derived from biology, may be found in the writings of Miller (1955) and Stogdill (1959). Systems theories place major emphasis on various kinds of 'input and output' of the system, and they share with field theory a fundamental interest in equilibrating processes.

4. *Sociometric orientation.* Originated by Moreno (1934) and elaborated by Jennings (1943), this is concerned primarily with the interpersonal choices that bind groups of people together. The remarkably large quantity of research conducted within this orientation has been effectively reviewed by Lindsey and Borgatta (1954), who point out that little systematic theory has yet resulted.

5. *Psychoanalytic theory.* Psychoanalytic theory focuses upon certain motivational and defensive processes within the individual and was first extended to group life by Freud (1922). In more recent years, especially as a result of the growing interest in group psycho-therapy, it has been elaborated in various ways by such writers as Bach (1954), Bion (1948-50, 1952), Ezriel (1950), Scheidlinger (1952), and Stock and Thelen (1958). Of special relevance to group dynamics are its concepts of identification, regression, defence mechanisms and the unconscious. Although comparatively little experimental or quantitative research on groups has been conducted within this orientation, concepts and hypotheses from psychoanalytic theory have permeated much of the work in group dynamics.

6. *General psychology orientation.* Since groups consist of individuals, it is to be expected that conceptions of human behaviour developed in general psychology will be found in work on group dynamics. And, in fact, the influence of each of the major theories of motivation, learning and perception can be seen. Perhaps the most influential of these to date has been a broad approach referred to as cognitive theory. This is not, strictly speaking, a theory but a point of view that insists on the importance of understanding how individuals receive and integrate information about the social world and how this information affects their behaviour. Important contributions to the study of groups have been made within this orientation by Asch (1952), Festinger (1957, ch.10), Heider (1958) and Krech and Crutchfield (1948).

7. *Empiricistic statistical orientation.* This maintains that the concepts of group dynamics should be discovered from statistical procedures, such as factor analysis, rather than constructed on a priori grounds by a theorist. Those working in this orientation make considerable use of the procedures developed in the field of personality testing. Good illustrations of this approach may be found in the writings of Borgatta, Cottrell and Meyer (1956), Cattell (1948) and Hemphill (1956) who have concentrated to date on ascertaining the orthogonal dimensions in terms of which groups can be characterized.

8. *Formal models orientation.* In sharp contrast to this last orientation is the work of a group of writers who have attempted to construct formal models with the aid of mathematics in order to deal rigorously with some rather limited aspects of groups. Although these models ordinarily contain some assumptions drawn from one or another of the social sciences, the emphasis is more on formal rigor than on comprehensive substantive theory. Examples of this approach may be found in publications of French (1956), Harary (1959), Hays and Bush (1954), Rapaport (1963) and Simon (1957).

Nobody in his senses sets out to use a tool or instrument without ensuring as far as possible that the tool he selects has apparently some, if not all, the qualities that he thinks appropriate to the task in hand. Of course, there are several areas of potential error here:

1) He may not know precisely what kind of task faces him or be mistaken in his assumptions (the task may be larger, smaller, or different in kind from what he sees it to be).

2) He may not know the qualities of the tool or its appropriateness for the task, or again he may be mistaken in any of the assumptions he makes about it.

There are two major ways of resolving this dilemma. The first and most common is to rely on judgements, usually based on past experience and similarities, and to try or to reject on this basis. The second is much more scientific and involves research into the nature of the factors involved in the hope that increased understanding will result.

When the factors involved are human behaviour and methods of effecting changes in behaviour consciously and directed to some specific end, these means of resolving the dilemma of what to do become fraught with difficulties not found in dealing with situations not directly concerned with human behaviour. For instance, there arises the question of not only whether such a method will achieve a particular end, but also whether the method is morally justifiable. There are several ways of changing behaviour which are probably quite effective and relatively easy, but which have seldom been used because they offend against human dignity, e.g. enforced sterility, punishing by disfigurement (chopping off the hands of thieves, putting out the eyes of spies, etc.), generally by rendering a person incapable of pursuing a particular line of previous behaviour.

Man has always sought for more effective ways of changing the behaviour of others. Seldom has he sought for ways to change his own behaviour. What usually emerges from this search is that change which is enforced may be effective, but it usually requires the ongoing expenditure of costly resources to maintain, so that it becomes uneconomic in the long term. Change if it is to be effective needs to be change willingly ascribed to by the persons who are expected to change, for then no enforcement is necessary only encouragement. As long as any person sees his best interests being served by maintaining a certain pattern of behaviour it will tend to continue.

One of the tools or instruments that is used in attempts to alter human behaviour is the group situation. Social scientists have examined the effects of this instrument on some areas of human behaviour in minute detail. Much of their work is of great interest to the student of human behaviour, but it lacks a theoretical framework which would link each piece with the others. This lack destroys much of the practical use such research would otherwise have. Others have assumed that the instrument is valid, a decision based upon empirical evidence, and have used it to effect change in human behaviour.

Inevitably in this kind of situation, such is the need for an effective instrument of change, that practice outstrips the theoretical proof of effectiveness, and observational criteria of change in relatively uncontrolled situations are accepted as justification for continuing and expanding practice. This creates a traditional base for practice, rather than a theoretical one. It is the purpose here to endeavour to examine this received wisdom, not so much to question it - for there is little to put in its place - but to make it more explicit.

The most basic of all the assumptions that group workers make is of the fundamental nature of group experience.

The Fundamental Nature of Group Experience

'Deep within every man there lies the dread of being alone in the world, forgotten by God, overlooked among the tremendous household of millions and millions. That fear is kept away by looking upon all those about one who are bound to one as friends or family, but the dread is nevertheless there and one hardly dares think of what would happen to one of us if all the rest were taken away.' (Kirkegaarde, 1938).

'Even the membership of the most pitiable of human communities, a group of dope addicts, can seem to some preferable to isolation.' (Lorenz, 1969).

In order that much of what follows may come into clear perspective, it is essential to realize the dependent state of all human beings; dependent that is upon each other. Koestler calls this dependence 'one of the central features of the human predicament' and describes it as an 'overwhelming capacity and need for identification with a social group and/or a system of beliefs which is indifferent to reason, to self-interest and even to the claims of self-preservation' (1969).

Clearly, without succour a newborn infant will die. In order to reach a stage of development at which he would be self-sufficient, such an infant has to go through a long period of dependence upon those able to nurture him. The whole process of maturation can be seen as a continuous interaction between the genetic endowment of the individual and the environment which surrounds him. This is a flexible arrangement and leads to individuality, but the common elements of experience and endowment are sufficient to create recognizable similarities within given areas where the over-all patterns of experience are alike.

Kingsley Davis says 'No sharp line can be drawn between our own selves and the selves of others, since our own selves function in our experience only in so far as the selves of others function in our experience also'. Again when he is talking about 'me' he writes 'since it is built out of the attitudes of others, the self cannot help but place a value on these attitudes apart from, or in spite of, organic satisfaction' (1947: 554-65). George H. Mead describes how a child's personality is developed in relation to 'significant others', i.e. members of his family or other primary groups such as the playgroup. Mead did not actually use the term 'group', he wrote of 'others' and the 'social world', but he was talking about group situations and their effect on the maturing child (1934).

Man has long recognized his dependence on others. The most terrible of punishments he has devised have, almost without exception, contained some element of isolation or banishment. In small early communities, expulsion was almost certainly a sentence of death unless some other group could be established outside the prohibited area. Periods of prolonged withdrawal from contact with other human beings produce disturbances of physical and mental functioning, even when the withdrawal is voluntary and the knowledge that a return can be made at any time is present. The men who attempt to break records by staying in mines or potholes without human contact become disorientated despite conditions which are otherwise reasonable. Finally, in the process of establishing the effects of sensory deprivation, researchers have noted the disturbing effects, both physical and mental, which prolonged isolation from human, or other contact, have upon the subjects of their experiments.

Each individual can now be seen as the product of an ongoing process of interaction, but the basis of his individual personality has been established by the interactions of his early years, particularly with those closest to him, both physically and affectionately. This does not make him a pre-conditioned automaton, for he can learn from his experience and control his behaviour to some extent, but his future is not entirely unplotted and in any case his dependence upon others will tend to shape its main outlines.

Group experience is therefore universal, but obviously of different qualities, intensities, and duration; it is also a multiple experience in that most people are subjected to being members of many groups at the same moment in time, though perhaps not actually physically present in more than one at any given instant. But without question our experience in each of these groups has some effect upon our behaviour in any or all of the others. This had led T.M. Mills to say that there is no such thing as a 'closed' group, i.e. a group with a fixed and permanent membership, because even such a group is subject to the influence of other groups and the society at large in which it exists, the influence being imported by the members as part of their experience into the so-called 'closed' group.

The idea that man is dependent runs through many disciplines and forms a counter to excessive concentration upon the individual as an existing entity. Some of the strongest expressions of the interdependent state can be found in the writings of the role theorists like Mead, already quoted, and Cooley. Berger maintains that this viewpoint challenges 'one of the fondest pre-suppositions about the self - its continuity' (1963: 124-5).

He sees that this indicates that the self is rather 'a process, continuously created and recreated in each social situation that one enters, held together by the slender thread of memory' (1963).

Cooley writing about 'primary groups' said

'What else can human nature be than a trait of primary groups? Surely not an attribute of the separate individual - supposing there were any such thing — since its typical characteristics, such as affection, ambition, vanity and resentment, are inconceivable apart from society: If it belongs then to men in association, what kind or degree of association is required to develop it? Evidently nothing elaborate, because elaborate phases of society are transient and diverse, while human nature is comparatively stable and universal. In short, the family and neighbourhood life is essential to its genesis and nothing more is' (1929: 23).

The same idea in a slightly different form can be found in Malinowski's work; in writing about the basic nature of the concept of 'group' in sociology he says 'Nor can such conceptions as individual, personality, self or mind be described except in terms of membership in a group or groups - unless again we wish to hug the figment of the individual as a detached, self-contained entity'. Later he points out that in a functional analysis of a society 'individuals never cope with or move within, the environment in isolation, but in organised groups, and that organisation is expressed in traditional charters, which are symbolic in essence' (1939: 938).

So much stress is laid upon the influence of the group in society by some sociologists that, as Berger says, they are in danger of presenting 'an image of society as a forbidden person'. This is in the sense that the ability of an individual to influence his destiny and behaviour is curtailed in all directions by the 'prohibitions of society and the expectations of the others around him'. However, he also points out that the individual has some freedom within the constraints imposed by society and also that he develops consistent patterns of behaviour which are long lasting and relatively stable, even to the point of resisting externally expected change.

In another area of attempted understanding of human behaviour, psychiatry, where the influence of medicine has until recently stressed the value of the individual as a clinical entity, the work of Laing and others shows an awareness of the interdependent state of man. In *The Divided Self* he says

'Unless we begin with the concept of man in relation to other men and from the beginning "in" a world, and unless we realise that man does not exist without "his" world, nor can his world exist without him, we are condemned to start our study of schizoid and schizophrenic people with a verbal and conceptual splitting that matches the split up of the totality of the schizoid being-in-the-world' (1959: 19-20).

One final quotation from Laing, which seems to have the essence of man's interdependent state summed up within it because it includes also the concept of isolation, will now be given:

'There is another aspect of man's being which is the crucial one in psychotherapy as contrasted with other treatments. This is that each and every man is at the same time separate from his fellows and related to them. Such separateness and relatedness are mutually necessary postulates. Personal relatedness can exist only between beings who are separate but who are not isolates. We are not isolates and we are not parts of the same physical body. Here we have the paradox, the potentially tragic paradox, that our relatedness to others is an essential aspect of our being, as is our separateness, but any particular person is not a necessary part of our being' (1959: 26).

Ogden Nash is a writer of humorous verse. Like a great many humorists he is fully aware of human tragedy - our inability to communicate effectively with each other. He wrote in *Listen:*

There is a knocking in the skull
An endless silent shout
Of something beating on a wall
And crying, 'Let me out'.

The solitary prisoner
Will never hear reply,
No comrade in eternity
Can hear the frantic cry.

No heart can share the terror
That haunts his monstrous dark;
The light that filters through the chinks
No other eye can mark.

When flesh is linked with eager flesh
And words run warm and full,
I think that he is loneliest then,
The captive in the skull.

Caught in a mesh of living veins,
In cell of padded bone,
He loneliest is when he pretends
That he is not alone.

We'd free the incarnate race of man
That such a doom endures
Could only you unlock my skull
Or I creep into yours.

Much of the impact of others upon our lives is difficult to
describe in terms of group activity unless the term is used in its
very widest sense. But in view of the fact that the essential basis
of group existence is interaction between members, then, in the
course of existing, people interact with others at many different
levels of intensity and for longer or shorter periods. It is possible
to suggest that the patterns of human relationships are
essentially three: the isolate, which is a non-relationship; the
dyad, the relationship of two people; and the triad, the
relationship of three people. There seems to be some evidence
that human groups larger than three tend to display combinations
of these three basic patterns, and the relationship between the
parts need not be constant. Changing structures, for instance,
which bring differing needs may be met by different constellations
within the group, but regularly occurring situations will end to be
met in a consistent way.

The basic orientation then is that of the essential nature of
group existence and the interdependence of mankind. This
stresses that the 'group' is fundamental in society, any society,
and thus when discussing the nature of a group it is not meant
that the discussion is about an 'artificially' created entity, but
about a natural phenomenon. This postulate has some dangers
as can be seen from the discussion of the definition of a group,
mainly in the sense that researchers do tend to study 'created'
groups. The danger lies in extrapolating to the more natural
groupings of mankind findings that are only relevant to created

groups. If research had concentrated the other way, this particular danger would have been almost negligible.

The universality of group experience creates difficulties in isolating for study various areas of group influence on the individual. Thus in a most general way group experience affects nearly every aspect of an individual's life. This is repeated in a encouragement of each member to participate according to the area of study is related to every other area known about. If one factor is altered, say size, by the addition of another member, then in a small group of the kind under consideration every other factor is influenced by the change in one way or another.

Again the universality of group experience is demonstrated in any consideration of the effect of group influence on an individual. Studies have been made in the areas of conformity, conflict, power, values, and standards, the way in which people do all manner of things, and the power of sanctions. The degree to which choice is left for the individual is a matter of great debate, for the ways in which he sees the choices, or even whether he sees them at all, may well be markedly influenced by the group pressures to which he is subject.

'Unpleasant as the realisation may be to egotists, very few individuals can be considered as more than incidents in the life histories to which they belong. Our species long ago reached the point where organised groups rather than their individual members became the functional units in its struggle for survival.' (Ely Chinoy, 1968).

'For better or for worse, the individual is always and forever a member of groups. It would appear that no matter how 'autonomous' and how 'strong' his personality, the commonly shared norms, beliefs, and practices of his group bend and shape and mould the individual.' (Krech, Crutchfield and Ballachey, 1962: 486).

G. Konopka offers a list of what she calls the 'Principles of some group work in practice', and also of the 'Theories of man underlying social group'. Combined, these compilations give a kind of survey of most of the basic assumptions that group workers appear to make about the work they do.

Principles of Social Group Work in Practice

Group work practice is based on an optimism that assumes that the human being can be helped to grow and change. It is not a romantic optimism, but one that drives toward action - a realistic idealism.

Its three premises are:

i) Social work as a profession is concerned with the enhancement of people's social functioning.

ii) There is significant correlation between social functioning and group experience.

iii) People need help — sometimes professional help — to enhance social functioning.

Out of philosophy, knowledge, and skill evolve fourteen basic principles of social group work:

1) recognition and subsequent action in relation to the unique difference of each individual

2) recognition and subsequent action in relation to the wide variety of groups as groups

3) genuine acceptance of each individual with his unique strengths and weaknesses

4) establishment of a purposeful relationship between group worker and group member

5) encouragement and enabling of help and co-operative relationships between members

6) appropriate modification of the group process

7) encouragment of each member to participate according to the stage of his capacity and enabling him to become more capable

8) enabling of members to involve themselves in the process of problem solving

9) enabling group members to experience increasingly satisfactory forms of working through of conflicts

10) provision of opportunities for new and differing experience in relationships and accomplishments

11) judicious use of limitations related to the diagnostic assessment of each individual and the total situation

12) purposeful and differential use of programme according to diagnostic evaluation of individual members, group purpose, and appropriate social goals

13) ongoing evaluation of individual and group progress

14) warm human and disciplined use of self on the part of the group worker.

In an analysis of practice we can observe these principles in action. We see the importance of time in the helping process and the complicated net of interrelationships which the group worker must understand and with which he must work. The goal, help with social functioning, is not reached quickly or in a straight line, but often through several backward and forward movements.

Theories of Man Underlying Social Group Work

Group work practice is based on a concept of man as a constantly developing human being in necessary and significant interactions with other men. He is shaped by others and is shaping others. He presents an inseparable unit of physical, mental, and emotional facets, again in interaction with others.

Development does not cease with childhood, but continues all through the life cycle. The basic needs beyond the biological ones are the needs to belong, to be an important individual, and to participate.

In the life cycle these needs must be fulfilled in a variety of changing small group associations. These associations have specific characteristics in different age periods. At each stage of development individuals must find fulfilment through qualitative group associations or they will be damaged in one way or another. No individual goes through the life cycle without some damage. Human beings have various capacities to deal with dissatisfactions and frustrations on their own. They need help at different stages of their development with their developmental task or with overcoming hurdles to them. Group work practice is directed towards provision of such help.

Because of its strong emphasis on viewing the individual in interaction and therefore the importance of the qualitative group life, its practice is also based on a thorough understanding of the dynamics of face-to-face groups.

A healthy group life has the following ingredients:
1) provision for the identification with equals
2) provision for the warmth of belonging to more than one person. Fear of the threatened loss of the one and only beloved person

is always present and becomes overwhelming if a wider
relationship is not established in the course of life
3) freedom to be and to express oneself and to be different in
the presence of others
4) freedom to choose the friends one prefers combined with a
responsibility to accept others if they need to be accepted, even
though no close friendly relationship has been established
5) opportunity to try out our own individuality while at the
same time permitting the enjoyment of the uniqueness of others
6) opportunity to exercise independence and to be allowed to be
dependent when this is necessary and indicated, as in childhood
or in distressing situations in adulthood.

Konopka (1963: 39-40; 163; 167-70)

Basic Assumptions

It is now possible to draw up a list of the basic assumptions upon
which group work practice is founded. The experience of groups
is basic to human existence and current behaviour patterns have
been largely group-formed and should be modifiable to some
extent by controlled group exercise.

Basic Assumptions
1) that group experience is universal and an essential part of
human existence
2) that groups can be used to effect changes in the attitudes and
behaviour of individuals
3) that groups provide experiences which can be monitored or
selected in some way for beneficial ends. Life outside the group
is in no way neglected, it tends to be 'put out of focus' in favour
of considering the 'here and now' situation within the group
4) that groups offer experience shared with others so that all can
come to have something in common with the sense of belonging
and of growing together
5) that groups produce change which is more permanent than can
be achieved by other methods and change which is obtained more
quickly also
6) that groups assist in the removal or diminution of difficulties
created by previous exposure to the process of learning
7) that groups as instruments of helping others may be

economical in the use of scarce resources, e.g. skilled workers, time, etc.

8) that a group can examine its own behaviour and in so doing learn about the general patterns of group behaviour (process).

REFERENCES

Cartwright, D. and Zander, A. (1953) *Group Dynamics.* London: Tavistock.

Chinoy, E. (1968) *Sociological Perspective.* N.Y.: Random.

Davis, K. (1974) Final Note on a Case of Extreme Isolation. *American Journal of Sociology,* pp. 554-65. March.

Dru, Alexander (ed. and trans.) (1938) *The Journals of Kirkegaarde.* London: OUP.

Koestler, A. (1969) *The Place of Value in a World of Facts* Paper given at Stockholm.

Konopka, G. (1963) *Social Group Work.* Englewood Cliffs, N.Y.: Prentice Hall.

Krech, D., Crutchfield, R.S. and Ballachey, E. L. (1962) *The Individual in Society.* Montreal: McGraw Hill.

Laing, R.D. (1959) *The Divided Self.* London: Tavistock.

Lewin, K. (1951) *Field Theory in Social Science.* N.Y.: Harper and Row.

Lorenz, K. (1969) Paper given at Stockholm to Nobel Prizewinners.

Malinowski, B. (1939) The Group and the Individual in Functional Analysis. *American Journal of Sociology 44:* 938-46. May.

Mead, G.H. (1964) *Mind, Self and Society.* Chicago: University of Chicago Press.

Mills, T.M. (1964) *Group Transformation.* Englewood Cliffs, N.J.: Prentice Hall.

part 2

Practice theory

I

Introduction

'Practice Theory' is the kind of material that group practitioners have found empirically to be effective and have recorded for the benefit of others. Practice in most instances outstrips validation and certainly it is far in advance of any theorizing that takes place. Procedures are adopted and repeated because they are seen to work; different techniques and methods are tried because someone has a good idea and either old methods have been found wanting, or there was no 'old' method to deal with a particular situation.

There is one particular area where the empirical techniques have undoubted value and that is as a set of simple guidelines for those who want to work with groups.

Groupwork literature notoriously is not overblessed with precise information about the actual details of coping with the problems of handling a group of people. Admittedly the most effective method of learning groupwork skills is a kind of apprenticeship with a skilled practitioner, so that the first fumbling steps can be taken in the knowledge that there is help immediately available as well as instruction and support. But this is no real reason why the accumulated wisdom of many group·practitioners should not be made available for those who need it.

Much reporting of group work, especially in the social work

field, has two major faults: 1) the hard data about such things as why the group was set up (e.g. how were the members recruited, how long did it last, where were meetings held, what kind of leadership was involved, how was it recorded, what kind of experience had the leader, how was it evaluated etc.) never seem to be offered, or if there is some attempt to cover these points some of the more relevant ones are omitted; 2) the amount of descriptive material and opinion-giving is usually far too great. Theoretical orientations of the writers are rarely given and the whole tends to camouflage the lack of really hard facts which would be of inestimable value to those who are seeking for help in their own groupwork practice.

Another factor is that the written material does not often coincide with the observed needs of beginners in this field. The absolutely concrete data of running a group tend to be omitted in favour of stating information which is peripheral.

This section, then, attempts to remedy the problem just outlined and to provide, as far as possible, data which should enable any person interested in groups to have a clearer idea about what may be termed the 'mechanics' of groupwork practice.

The material offered here has been culled from many sources and starts with a consideration of *Preparation.* There is mounting evidence to indicate that one of the major reasons why groups 'go wrong' is that insufficient attention has been given to the preparatory period. Perhaps the current climate of opinion about groups is largely responsible. Many social agencies involve themselves and their staffs in groupwork either because they feel that they are getting on a bandwagon, or because they feel that there must be a correlation between one person dealing with a number of people at one time and economies of resources and time. There is some possible justification, although not much, for the second belief, but none at all for the first. Just as a house or any building is only as secure as its foundations, a group may well be only as effective as the preparation upon which it is based.

The material on *Preparation* is followed by a consideration of the concept of 'Contract'. In many ways this is an idea new to social work but not new either to business or some branches of the medical profession. 'Contract' is based upon several well-known facts, the foremost of which is that of participation and the consequent easing of anxiety.

Many practitioners have long been concerned about the number of people who drop out of treatment for no very clear reasons. Others have been concerned about the admittedly scarce feedback from consumers of treatment and resources. Both these factors may well be underwritten by the apparent assumption that if clients are informed that what is about to take place is good for them, then their faith in the integrity, professional skill, and honesty of the practitioner will enable them not only to accept what is offered, but also to benefit by it.

Evidence abounds to show that this kind of faith does not exist in abundance, but that it can be engendered. To create it the practitioner needs to realize that what to him may be obvious, logical, and indisputably good reasons for proceeding in the way he suggests may not appear so to his clients. His familiarity with the processes, his training, and the way he thinks may blind him to the fact that his clients may well see things differently. This kind of discrepancy can be illustrated by an analogy with games. In this sense the practitioner and his clients are in the position of a group of people who are about to play a very difficult and skilled game when only one person, the groupworker in this case, is knowledgeable about the rules or has had any practice in this particular game. The rest have played games with some degree of similarity to this one, but *they do not know the rules.* Most people play with more confidence and with greater involvement and commitment when they know either what the rules are or that they have a chance to modify them to their advantage whenever they wish. 'Contract' is concerned with a method of involving clients directly, consciously, and with understanding in the group process.

Any person who becomes involved in working with groups becomes involved in the way in which groups are led. There is more literature about the concepts of leadership than any other aspect of group behaviour. Obviously the problem of leading others has been with us since the beginning of man's existence. But all group practitioners have to face the fact that if they are going to work with their groups they will be, in the majority of cases, designated leaders, i.e. imposed upon others. This makes for some difficulties about authority and dependency, but it is also closely tied up with the concepts of responsibility and accountability.

The section on leadership attempts to clarify some of the issues involved. For instance, leadership is inextricably bound up with the developmental life of a group. In the early stages of a group the leader may have been responsible for calling the group together; his responsibility does not therefore cease at the moment of the group's convening unless his group is formed expressly to consider the problems of leadership. But this does not mean either that his responsibility will not change. As a group grows and learns to work together, the character of the leadership it needs will change and indeed leaders may well emerge from within the group. From this point of view any designated leader needs to be sensitive to the changing expectation of his group and to adapt himself accordingly.

Obviously the problem of 'how many leaders?' is bound to occur and so this section also looks to the co-leader situation and at the role of the resource person as well. Here the real deficiency of the written or spoken word to convey the skills of leadership is very manifest and the realities of leadership can only be clearly worked through by constant practice in the role with different groups.

It has been said elsewhere in this book that all the factors of a group's existence which may be isolated for examination, have, in practice, a complex interdependent relationship one with another. Alter one by deliberate intervention and in some degree most of the others will change too. The size of a group has been one such factor frequently used as an experimental variable because of the ease of control. However, there are certain simple facts related to the size of any given group, mostly of a common sense nature, which are of value to the group practitioner. The section on size attempts to present these facts as simply as possible.

Very few people are trained observers. Most of us 'look' at things, people, situations; but few of us can be said to 'see' what we look at. Familiarity causes us to accept without question complex interactions and seldom to remember what occurred. Take the making of decisions. If a group of people, friends, family, workmates perceive that they have a problem (it will be fortunate if they all perceive it, and more fortunate if they all perceive they have the same problem - but highly unlikely), a solution may be found and action taken, but unless the decision-making process was glaringly obvious, e.g. autocratic direction by one powerful person - few members of that group will have seen what happened. Convention pushes us away from the observation of our own behaviour and the actions of others.

However, as has been stated, if the group practitioner hopes to be able to use group processes for beneficial ends, then not only he, but every member of the group has to be encouraged to notice what is going on. An individual or a group has no control over processes of which he is unaware, so it must obviously be an increment of personal growth to decrease the number of processes wherein he is denied the right to choose his *stand* by virtue of ignorance.

Good observing may come to nothing if it is not well recorded. Over a period of time the ability to compare observations must lead to an increase in understanding of the processes of the group. Recording a group's interaction is a difficult process simply because the interaction is complex and involves many factors; because the group leader is usually not just a passive recorder but also actively engaged as an influential member of the group. This section aims to present simple to complex methods of recording, to detail some of the instruments used and also to give some guidance toward an understanding of the more common phenomena which may be observed.

Co-operation within groups frequently seems to be accepted as the goal to be achieved. Human behaviour is seldom totally co-operative and to attempt to achieve such in created groups may well lead to a form of apathy and stagnation. Conflict is essential to human existence, to ambition, and to devising new methods of coping. In most groups, which are after all small versions of real life, conflict is equally essential. The purpose of a given group may call for more co-operation than conflict or more of one at one period of its life and more of the other at some other time. 'Purpose dictates practice' is true in all aspects of groupwork.

The possibilities of conflict are looked at within this section and consideration given to the resolution of conflict, the harnessing of conflict for progress, and the creation of conflict for benefit to the group as a whole. To bring conflict into the open may be the aim of setting up a confrontation between members. Some conflicts drain energy that the group can ill

afford to lose. This is especially so when the conflicts are hidden
or unacknowledged.

The behaviour of groups is the behaviour of the members of
the group. One of the most frequent questions that newcomers
to group practice ask is 'when does a collection of people become
a group?'. In this section the roles which members occupy; the
contribution they make to group life; the concept of
followership i.e. the role/function of follower; and the various
partnerships which can arise are presented. In many ways this is
the most difficult section in that the interaction of members of a
group is the basic process and it is very complex. By splitting off
bits of this process to look at some, loss of reality is inevitably
experienced with subsequent difficulty in relating the parts to
the whole.

Groups are living organisms, having a beginning, and a middle,
and an end. The development of a group is not simply in a straight
line, or even a simple parabola, but tends to go in a series of
forward movements interspersed with regressive interludes. The
general movement, if the group is healthy, is toward its avowed
goal despite the backward periods. Perhaps the most frequent
cause of regressive movement is the threat which exposure to
other people tends to produce, and the corollary to this, is the
development of trust among the group members, which pushes a
group toward its goal. Thus some consideration of the generation
and effect of these two factors is essential to an over-all appreciation of the way in which groups function.

Some groups definitely create a climate in which their members
work well together; some groups never seem to achieve this; still
others, the majority in fact, fluctuate between the two poles.
The study of the threat and trust elements can really only be
made in the light of the general climate in which the group
operates. Some factors which help the group create a good
working climate will also be considered.

The very important issue of ending a.group is left almost to
the end, so that it can be seen as a process which is utterly
dependent upon everything that has gone before. It is in a very
real sense as much the running down of a structure as preparation
is the creation of one. Termination is fraught with problems and
is too often ignored on the false assumption that if a car is not
driven it will stop.

This section ends with a glossary of the main terms used in the practice of groupwork. The basic assumption here is that a fundamental understanding of the terminology will enable sense to be made out of texts on the subject area which tend to be heavily laden with somewhat confusing jargon. No claim is made for any profundity or depth in the analysis of the groupwork terms, an attempt has merely been made at rendering them intelligible to the newcomer.

2

Preparation

There is only one sufficient reason for using group techniques
in a social situation, which is that in the considered opinion of the
group convenor it is by all available data the best possible means
of coping with the social situation. This means that as many as
can be of the factors influencing the situation will be considered
before any decision to use a group approach is taken.

This leads directly to the formation of a basic purpose for
any convened groups, e.g. to sort out a particular problem, to
offer opportunities for social contact; to perform a co-operative
operation, and so on. Many groups seem to be formed by
well-meaning people who appear to start from the notion
'Wouldn't it be a good idea if we were to put all these people
into a group?' probably because there are several people with
similar problems. The underlying aim would seem to be to
facilitate the task of the worker by seeing several people at once
and not that grouping those people would provide the best
approach to whatever their problem may be. Some of the main
reasons for using a group approach may be listed as follows:
1) there is already a 'group' problem.
2) to use peer learning, e.g. Alcoholics Anonymous.
3) to make beneficial use of group pressures.
4) to make beneficial use of interpersonal interaction.

5) to make beneficial use of the support system of a group.
6) to make beneficial use of the social nature of group meetings.
7) to make beneficial use of the resources of the group.

A fundamental value of being a group member is shared experience. The distinction between being a member of a given group and not being a member is that each individual has or has not shared some part of his experience with others. The problem of newcomers to established groups is precisely this. However similar their experience may be they have not experienced it in the company of the group members they are now joining. The creation of a group is basically the act of providing a situation in which a given number of people can have the opportunity of having certain experiences together.

The task of preparing for a group is not simple. In fact the future of any group largely depends upon the soundness of the preparation which was made for its creation. A simple list of what is involved would be as follows:

1) a social situation is seen to exist which would appear to respond to a group approach
2) a basic aim for such a group can be formulated
3) the resources (material and otherwise) exist
4) forecasts of type of group, activity, duration, frequency, etc., can be made
5) members can be selected on clear criteria.

This can be set out as a simple planning programme:

Table 2 Planning Programme For Starting a Group
Purpose

Type of Group
Method
Programme
Place
Duration   *Frequency*
                                              Time

Members

      i) Selection
     ii) Age range
   iii) Sex distribution
   iv) Numbers
    v) Other criteria

Theoretical Base

Other Factors

To take into consideration as many factors as possible before the group is actually convened means clearing ideas to the point that a groupworker has got a reasonable certainty about what he intends to do. This can only be beneficial especially when contracts are made for the simple reason that the groupworker may be faced with the task of 'selling' what he has to offer to a relatively disbelieving client. If his own ideas and values are hazy, then he will not be convincing.

A more complex check-list for starting a group is given here after a need which can be met by group methods has been established:

1) What type of group?
    a) leisure activities
    b) educational
    c) social treatment
    d) mixed
2) Method?
    a) play
    b) drama and role-play

c) talk

d) movement

e) work

f) total community

g) mixed

3) Where? (ensure that the place is suitable for the method and purpose and members)

4) How long will each session last?

5) How frequently will the group meet?

6) For how long?

7) At what time?

8) Is transport available, if necessary?

9) What kind of theoretical base is to be used? e.g. (groups facilitate communication)

10) What is the main purpose of the group?

11) How will members be selected?

a) on what basis

b) age range

c) sex distribution

d) how many

e) any other relevant factors

f) where will they come from e.g. social background

g) intelligence

h) ability to verbalize (if necessary)

12) Are there any secondary purposes?

13) Is it possible with the resources available?

14) If not, what is needed? Can it be obtained?

15) Does the proposed group fit into the department's policy?

16) How many group leaders will be needed? What roles will they play?

17) What style of group leadership is involved? e.g. permissive, directive, etc.

18) Will the sessions be recorded? What method will be used?

19) Are there facilities for consultation: a) with experts, b) with group leaders involved?

20) Will individual sessions be available for members as well? a) with whom? b) when?

21) Have you explained to your colleagues what you are trying to do?

One of the most practical problems facing a potential

groupworker may well be 'what kind of group'. There are several ways of classifying groups: according to their main activity, e.g. play groups, therapy groups, etc.; according to their style, e.g. permissive, authoritarian; according to their purpose, e.g. education, and so on. But the one factor that emerges clearly from most attempts at classification is that purpose tends to dictate the nature of the group.

Even this may be too simple, for it might be better to say that the nature of the group tends to be dictated by the way the purpose of the group is perceived. Obviously this introduces an element of discord, for not all the persons connected with a given group will see it existing for the same purpose. However, there are traditionally accepted kinds of groups which seem to be effective for certain purposes. The family as a group seems designed to serve the physical and emotional needs of parents and children and to facilitate the process of socialization into a given cultural pattern. There are alternatives, however, to the traditional family group which favour larger groupings or different kinds of relationships, e.g. the kibbutz.

Argyle in *Five Kinds of Small Groups* (1973: 240-66) discussed 'real life' groups much neglected by researchers because of the kind of problems mentioned earlier. (The problems referred to here are discussed in Part 1, Chapter 1, e.g. most data on groups comes from experimental groups not 'real' groups, i.e. groups set up for some purpose other than research). He draws attention to the fact that there are obvious differences between the groups he describes: the family; the adolescent friendship group; work groups; committees; problem-solving and creative groups; and finally T-groups and therapy groups - the main differences lying in the primary purpose of the group.

However, Argyle points to the fact that interaction in family groups is more complex and subtle than in most other groups, largely because of the kind of relationships which exist between members of a family. He lists four features present in family groups which are absent in other small groups:
1) a formal role structure whose pattern is defined by the culture
2) little self-presentation, but greater intimacy and intensity of interpersonal feelings
3) extra bonds exist, romantic love, parent/child relationship, blood ties, etc.

4) the duration of the family group covers many years and changing forms.

For those who would work with the family as the 'unit of service' rather than the individual or the larger community, such differences existing in the family group must be taken into account when attempting to apply general group theory. To take just one point as an example: any attempt to change the roles within a family group in order to meet changed circumstances and to enhance family functioning must take cognizance of the fact that family roles are defined by the culture and the pressures working against change may be very great, according to the kind of culture. The sense of being different is less easily coped with in such circumstances than changing roles within a work group for instance.

Within the adolescent friendship group, Argyle indicates that conformity to the group norms is perhaps the most striking feature. The need to establish an identity different from that created in the family group and the need to regulate behaviour and to support each other in acquiring competence in sexually oriented behaviour creates a tightly knit group. These factors are relevant to the group worker who chooses the adolescent gang as his area of activity and should condition his application of group theory, e.g. in relation to the ways in which such a group might be prepared to accept him and the values that he might be perceived as possessing.

Argyle then leaves the area of 'natural groups' and discusses purposes, with all the changes in emphasis that this change brings. The main factor is an increase in formal organization, and in committees the main task is problem-solving, and the accepted method is verbal interaction. There is much of interest here for the group worker especially in terms of the way a group works within boundaries which are formally set and acknowledged and how much depends upon the quality and motivation of committee members.

The final section deals with the T-group and therapy group, which as Argyle says 'did not exist until psychologists invented it'. These groups are usually the ones which are used as models by those aspiring to groupwork, and there are many dangers inherent in this attitude in that, as Klein's classification shows (see pp. 47,

49), many valuable group activities do not fall into the social treatment category.

It is therefore expedient that the basis of this kind of group should be considered at some length.

Group Experience

One of the ways of classifying groups, which has been mentioned previously, is by purpose. Thus, the kind of experience which a group may be designed to give its members can be used as an indication of purpose. Experience in this context is seen as a learning process and the end product is some degree of change in those involved in the process.

What is at issue is that, in being born and growing up, we are adjusting at some level to the society in which we exist. This tends to mean that we are equipped with patterns of social behaviour which that society regards as tolerable. These patterns include the way we react to others.

In order to produce even minimal conformity to these essentially imposed but eventually self-perpetuating patterns, each individual must learn to suppress other possible patterns of behaviour which he has discovered are socially invalid. The tragedy of this process, which is a product of community existence, is that it facilitates social intercourse at one level by inhibiting it at another. By this monitoring procedure, not only what is socially non-acceptable is filtered out, but also behaviour which is different. Thus, while ensuring the smooth functioning of society, this process encapsulates the individual in a cocoon of prohibitions, many of which he is unaware.

This may lead to a diminution of the potential behaviour of the individual and limit his responses to a small part of his total possible range. The excluded and ignored part of this range tends to be touched upon only when circumstances beyond the ordinary break through the encapsulating barrier of social training and elicit responses that are distinctly unusual and unfamiliar. These responses are almost always frowned upon by society and if not visited with some form of sanction are absorbed within a structure and made harmless.

A society may be said to facilitate behaviour patterns that are not only regarded as 'normal' but also as 'natural' and the problems of relationship which arise from such patterns seem to be of two basic kinds. First, there are those who, for some reason or other, cannot, or will not, accept the current socialization processes; and second, there are those who are faced with the demands of new and different situations calling for abilities and behaviours which may never have been needed before, or which have been suppressed in a socialization process which inevitably lags behind the needs of a developing society.

In the first situation the people concerned have not accepted the training process which would have adapted them to their society. At some stage, or at several, the process of social training has failed, or has been perverted and the end result is an individual with less than, or more than, the 'normal' adaptation to the ordinary demands of his society. Examples of this are legion and a great number of such apparently maladapted people can be contained within the structure of society, some proving useful as innovators and others needing constant care, control, or protection.

The second situation occurs to individuals and groups where previous adjustment has been within the normally accepted range, but where a demand now occurs for patterns of behaviour, perceptions, and abilities to relate, which have been outside the habitual range, e.g. organizational changes, the development of special skills and increased awareness and understanding. Some such situations arise quickly, others are the result of long periods of development in a given direction, when there is a gradual realization that new kinds of human resources or extensive realignments of old ones are required.

The latter situation implies that in some areas of social development the traditional, slowly evolving patterns of adjustment are outstripped by circumstances and need to be supplemented by consciously applied techniques to modify adaptive behaviour more rapidly to meet changing conditions. Some individuals become aware of the need to change and consciously attempt to adapt so that they can move with and into the developing areas. In most cases the cost is high because of the conflict between the new patterns of behaviour and the older habitually accepted patterns.

Some of this cost may be said to be in the distribution of energy, that is, the energy devoted to suppressing previous behaviour cannot also be directed to enhancing new behaviour. Thus the object of any technique employed to cope with this problem would be an attempt to free some of the energy devoted to maintaining habitual ways of seeing and behaving for productive use. Such techniques would seek to bring about a reassessment of habitual patterns of perception of the way others behave and the apparent causes of such behaviour, and create an experiential learning situation with the potential productive realignment of individual resources as its goal.

Obviously this requires that the individuals be confronted with others in a situation where such learning can take place. Thus the group must be the unit used. P. B. Smith (1971) discussed three kinds of group with the objective just described, directed to the enhancement of personal relationships and through these to increased self-fulfilment, greater understanding, and more effective working relationships.

A Classification

Some ideas have already been stated concerning the classification of groups according to different criteria. In this section a classification is offered which has the double merit of being simple and also workable. It is based upon the needs of social workers using group techniques, but it is nonetheless valuable for that. Perhaps its greatest omission lies in the fact that it is a classification of adult groups: children are nowhere mentioned. Klein (1961) gives four main areas in her classification:
i) Leisure-time groups
ii) Group education
iii) Social group treatment
iv) Group psychotherapy

Leisure-time groups are not considered at length here, though such groups based upon a given activity are perhaps the most common of created groups and are the kind of group which is most readily understood as such by people with little group experience. Indeed, clubs, team games, and social clubs are all so much a part of the social scene that there is very little difficulty in accepting them as groups.

What does become difficult is to gain the ability to see such loosely structured confederations of people as 'groups' in the sense that the behaviour exhibited in them shows some of the dynamics of more tightly structured groups and intervention by a group worker in such a situation is subjected to the same kind of strictures as are found in T-groups. On the whole, leisure groups are traditionally acceptable and their structure, particularly in clubs, of committees and officers is very well established. The essential factor which tends to bind members to the group is their common interest in the activity which is indulged in, or watched, or produced, etc.

In the section on group education, Klein's sub-categories are of special interest to social workers, but the over-all concept of using the group as a unit in education is of extreme importance. Certainly, there is considerable evidence to the effect that learning which takes place within a group situation and which the group accepts as the results of its own effort, rather than coming from without, is effective learning. A group using its own experience as a group to learn about groups is able usually to relate theoretical knowledge to practical experience very efficiently. The supportive effect of seeing others in the same state, of hearing their contributions, is much less threatening than the situation in which the individual maintains a relatively isolated competitive state.

The largest section is devoted to what Klein calls 'social group treatment', which concerns groups primarily created either to facilitate social functioning already apparent, or to modify functioning which tends to handicap the person concerned. In one case the group acts as a reinforcement-enhancing process, and in the other case acts as a touch-stone for its members in their attempts to modify maladaptive behaviour.

The distinction between education and treatment in a group situation is not always very distinct, for treatment frequently consists of a form of education or re-education, and education, when effective, can have marked effects upon adaptive behaviour.

Finally it might be said that some such classification as Klein's is necessary in order to clarify a somewhat confused situation and also to offer a logical choice to anyone interested in working with groups.

Klein's full classification is given below:

Table 3 Type of Group (according to Klein's classification)

I   Leisure-Time Groups

II   Group Education
                i) Family life education groups
                ii) Orientation groups
                iii) Re-intake groups

III   Social Treatment Groups
                i) Maintaining adaptive patterns
                ii) Modifying adaptive patterns

IV   Group Psychotherapy.

A working basis for the analysis of group activities is as follows:

Activity

For any of the types of groups referred to earlier there are probably any one or a combination of several of the following activities available to use.

1) Play - the use of games of all sorts, including playing with toys, sand, water, etc., in the case of children

2) Drama and Role-play - a specialized use of 'play' in which members of the group are asked to act various parts which have significance to the problems or difficulties of the group. The basic value of this kind of activity stems from the 'experiences' that it gives to groups and individuals of the way in which other people behave. It is also a very useful method by which individuals gain insight into their own behaviour and their relations to others. Moreno believed that there was great historical validity for this kind of activity.

3) Talk - this is the activity most people immediately associate with group activities, especially those of a 'treatment' nature. Included in this activity are lectures, discussions, seminars, conversations, etc. Obviously as an overemphasized mode of communication talk is an essential part of most of the other activities.

4) Movement - This kind of activity is being used as a counter to

the overemphasized or verbal communication just referred to. The activities include the exploration of touch, of non-verbal communication, dance, mime, and physical encounter.

5) Work - This activity speaks for itself and covers projects and tasks of all kinds of complexity which involve an ongoing process of co-operative endeavour.

6) Total Community - a rather strange 'activity' to include here as it is so many things at once. But it is the activity of group living with all that such a concept entails of being together for long periods of time.

An example of the combined use of several activities would be a club for young people which included within its over-all structure special groups. The social or leisure activity of the club would be its prime purpose, but within it discussion groups of all sorts could emerge. So, too, could work and drama groups.

Example

Groups have been increasingly used by probation workers and in penal institutions on the basis of either leisure activities, work groups, or as some form of treatment designed particularly to modify maladaptive behaviour patterns. In the field the problems are much the same as those faced by any other groupwork practitioner. There is the usual problem of attracting probationers to a group and of maintaining interest without necessarily resorting to the compulsory nature of a probation order.

But there are also problems that are specific to the practice of group work in this field. One of the major problems in this area concerns the use of groups within an institutional setting. Straight away the practitioner is forced to face the problem of where the groups he proposes to run fit within the institution. It is impossible to apply a group as a remedy to a situation in the same way as a pill or a plaster is applied. In every case the group becomes an integral part of the institution in which it is founded, influenced by it, and in turn influencing it. In this respect it becomes impossible to ignore the influence of the institution. Thus the kind of re-allocation of power that can take place within a democratic group must inevitably come to terms with any hierarchical power structure in the institution in which it exists. If freedom is promised to the group to make decisions which are incompatible with the structure of the organization, the decisions will be ineffective and the group will have received a powerful communication of its own helplessness. No group will work effectively in this situation.

Group Work in Probation by McCullough is concerned with a group of girls in a probation hostel. In this sense it is also concerned with one kind of residential groupwork with all the problems of selection, rejection, elites, and conflicting influences which this entails, and has been chosen because it illustrates these points clearly.

McCullough's group quite clearly had a large element of 'shared experience' in it, allied to a rather weaker element of 'personal growth'. She states that attendance was voluntary and that her interventions were few.

She was aiming at enhanced awareness on the part of the girls by creating a situation in which each girl would learn:
a) that she had common elements in her experience with other members of the group from which she would learn, and
b) that she could communicate with others and help them and receive help herself.

This group was oriented toward change and was largely a treatment group with the main activity being talk. This puts a premium on the ability to verbalize and the generation of a sense of trust, while the limitation of the group to small numbers created some problems for those who were excluded.

An analysis of McCullough's group, along nine principal parameters, would go as follows:

Figure 2 The Nine Parameters of Groupwork

TITLE OF ARTICLE: Groupwork in Probation

1. TYPE OF GROUP:

Leisure time	☐			
Group education	☐	Family life ☐	Orientation	☐
		Pre-Intake ☐		
Social treatment	☐	Maintenance ☐		
Group				
psychotherapy	☐	Modification ☐		

2. ACTIVITY:

Play	☐	Drama/role-play	☐	Talk	☑
Movement	☐	Work	☐	Total Community	☐

3. STATED AIM: To 'make contact' with delinquents

4. CLIENTELE:

Children	☐	Adolescents	☑	Adults	☑
Male	☐	Female	☑		
Coloured	☐	White	☐	Not-stated	☐

Other
All resident
in probation
hostel

5. PROBLEMS: —

6. SETTING: Probation hostel

7. SPECIAL TECHNIQUES: Selection - members volunteered in order of arrival at the hostel

8. STATED RESULTS: Facilitated relationship with worker, improved communication between members

9. COMMENTS: Individual sessions available with the group worker before and after group sessions.

It can be seen that this simple analysis forms the basis of the 'check list' for starting a group which can be found in this section. It should also be possible to use such an analysis to gain a better understanding of any written report on a group and to avoid the obscurity which much writing presents in this field. The simple facts of time, place, how long, when, method, etc., can either be easily listed or found to be not available. The example is therefore adjudged as useful or less useful according to the basic data revealed. McCullough describes the formation of her group in the following way:

'There is a growing amount of literature on the subject of group work and considerable divergence of aim and method, but there are certain basic requirements which are more or less common ground. It is generally considered that the group should consist of about seven or eight people. As few as five does not allow enough interrelationship to be significant and if there are as many as ten or eleven it is difficult for the worker to hold each member constantly in her attention, and for the group members to relate continually with one another. Chairs are placed in a rough circle, preferably with a table, and people left free to choose where they sit, the worker's position alone remaining constant. This allows the members of the group to sit in whatever position they choose in relation to the leader and to one another and to adopt the posture which suits their mood and to change it as their reactions change. This non-verbal communication is significant, particularly so in my setting because delinquents for various reasons are not usually going to verbalize easily.

Selection of group members is considered of primary importance by some workers in this field: whether people should be similar, because then they will have more in common, or different because this simulates the real life situation - or some particular combination of the two, like the Noah's Ark method by which two people are selected presenting each of several different problems, which allows each person to feel that they have something in common with at least one other in the group. For myself, I feel that human nature is so complex a thing that while I could match some characteristics - intelligence for example, or the offence committed - I have no way of knowing whether these aspects of the total situation are the vitally important ones, and prefer to take my group members in the order they arrive at the hostel, which in effect produces a mixed group.

Then there is the question of how the purpose is explained. With my groups I find it best to say very little, just that I think it sometimes helps them to talk over the problems they have in common. I give each girl the chance to refuse to come, although I only ever remember one doing so. The meetings last from an hour to an hour and a half and I begin to close them after an hour. I set a period to the group deliberately because in the delinquent authority situation people seem to tend to try and prolong a meeting which is due to close, whereas faced with an indefinite period of time they are more likely to resist with silence.

The groups meet weekly or bi-weekly on about six to ten occasions. This means in practice that a girl joins a group one to twelve weeks after her arrival at the hostel and stays in it for about three months. It will be appreciated that this is one of the critical times - the honeymoon period is over and people have not yet settled down. Before, during and after the group sessions I see the girls individually on an average of once every two weeks. My aim in the group is to deepen my relationship with the girls and to encourage real communication. The sort of group work that I do bears the same relation to group analysis that case work does to analysis - my aims are more limited and immediate and my interpretations rare and simple. I rely a great deal on the relief of tensions in the group, on the self understanding which is achieved when the girl herself puts into words perhaps for the first time in her life something that she feels deeply and finds that these feelings are understood, and often shared, by others and also on the 'reflected' relief and understanding they sometimes get from hearing a fellow member express something they feel themselves.

At first I tried to achieve these ends by being the passive, silent enigmatic leader of the classical group analytic situation. This puzzled and in a way frightened the girls who are used to me in a much more active role. I abandoned this attitude with reluctance only to find that the more I was willing to talk the less I was required to do so. My groups are now more or less leader-centred. In view of the total situation this would seem inevitable - and in fact has the advantage, because one of the ways in which the girls use the group is to come to terms with me as an authority figure, through this with authority generally, and so with their feelings about their parents.

In starting a session I make it clear that anything can be talked about and quite often they begin with a question - sometimes a very loaded one like 'Why are some girls sent to approved schools? If nothing comes spontaneously I attempt to stimulate, but not guide, discussion; that is I aim to get them to talk about almost anything because, once started, they will reach with surprising speed something that is important to them - more often than not their trouble with their parents, however unconnected this may seem to be with the original subject. If, on the other hand anti-authority feelings are rife at the time, the discussion will lead to these. Incidentally, they seldom feel able to express direct hostility to me or to something I have done in so many words, but they can bring it out quite recognizably by talking about probation officers generally, or police or magistrates, or by non-verbal communications. If this happens I play the game by their rules and offer generalized answers and explanations.'

Some groups are already in existence, e.g. families, gangs, etc. But most group workers will have to convene their own groups and this involves three major problems:

i) purpose
ii) selection
iii) initial contact

The setting in which the group is to be founded will influence all three. Thus, in a unit for addicts, the purpose is the major restorative purpose of the unit as a whole; selection may be based on availability, state of health, or willingness to take part; and the initial contact as made in a unit which has in some ways been preparing the client to meet the group as part of his treatment.

The most common purpose for establishing a group is that it will be supportive and create learning and growth situations for all its members. Usually this tends to dictate that the members have something in common. Frequently a common kind of problem is the basis for selection and also some commonly held aspiration to be helped in coping with it.

Where a common problem basis for a group exists then it is incumbent upon the group worker to select those he thinks will most benefit by being brought together. In many instances such groups are already selected because the number of people available is not vastly greater than the number considered desirable for the group. For instance where several people are seen to be facing change in their lives, there is likely to be anxiety which could be modified by their being members of a supportive group.

At the initial stages of any group the convenor has a special responsibility in that he alone knows really what is going on. To most people who may be drawn into the group such a procedure is outside their normal expectations; in other words the idea of using a group in these circumstances is strange. Thus the group leader has the duty to prepare himself to accept almost total responsibility for the group's existence and the basic establishment of norms. This kind of responsibility stems from the fact that the convenor will most probably have visited and talked to all the prospective group members. He will have discussed the formation of the group, the benefits that may be conferred upon the members, and the general aims which he sees as essential to the group at this time.

This tends to create a relationship in which every member of the proposed group knows the convenor. They have discussed with him their feelings about the proposed group and they have listened to the information he has to offer. This makes one factor all the members have in common apart from the problem - a relationship with the convenor - usually called in this context The Central Person (see section on *Leaders*).

There is mounting evidence that the single factor which is responsible for the breakdown of more groups than any other is lack of adequate preparation. Obviously preparation cannot take into consideration all the possible changes that may occur, but it *must* provide a secure basis from which to start. It is not possible to overstress the responsibility the convenor has to ensure that there is a need which can be met by the use of a group and to be certain that such a group bears a distinct and reality-based relationship to the environment in which it will function and that the resources are available. From this point on, sensitivity to the changing needs and development of the group is part of the skill of leadership and to adjust to these needs is a major factor in successful group leadership.

REFERENCES

Argyle, M. (1973) *Social Interaction.* London: Methuen
Klein, J.G. (1961) Social Group Treatment - Some Selected Dynamics. *In New Perspectives on Services to Groups.* New York:

National Association of Social Workers.

McCullough, M.K. (1963) Group Work in Probation In *New Society 21:* 9-11. 21 Feb.

Smith, P.B. (1971) Variety of Group Experience In *New Society.* 25 March.

3

The formation of contract

Hartford discusses a process which she calls 'setting a contract' in which the aims of a group of people are made explicit by discussion and a general agreement about the over-all or dominant purpose of the group can be settled.

However, the term 'contract' can be usefully seen to have a much wider application in groupwork practice. It can be used of the total and component arrangements, hidden or explicit, which members of the groups, leaders, and institutions make with each other.

What is implied in any group situation is that each member expects some level of satisfaction of his needs. If he does not get this level of satisfaction, then unless there are alternative satisfactions within the group situation, which are sufficiently compensatory, opting out will enhance his satisfactions more than staying and so he will leave. If practicable or possible then some form of withdrawal may take place within the group. One other move is possible, that of attempting to increase the possibility of meeting needs within the group by changing it in some way, by revolution, by sub-grouping, etc.

Almost without question a member of a group will remain actively within that group if it can be seen by him to be giving him some satisfaction greater than he could obtain elsewhere. Nothing is more likely to destroy his level of satisfaction than a conflict of expectations; that is when a member attends a group because he believes that it will meet certain of his felt needs and then becomes aware that such is not the case. Either the group aim in general is not what he thought it was, or his expectations of the group are different in some other way, or the group enhances certain dissatisfactions for the member disproportionately more than the satisfactions.

'Clearing expectations' is of fundamental importance in groupwork practice. It is not reasonable to suppose that, however much information has been given about the purpose of a group, or however much personal contact and preparation has been made, the individual members will assemble on the first meeting with common expectations. Such an assumption flies in the teeth of what is known about selective hearing and understanding and the way new information has to be related to previously accepted knowledge before it can be assimilated. Making explicit the expectations of the members of a group reveals many discrepant orientations - others may still remain hidden. 'Clearing expectations' becomes a method of establishing a working contract which is explicit or at least more explicit than the general assumptions which may otherwise have formed a relatively chaotic basis of operations.

'Contract' is defined as 'mutual agreement between two or more parties that something shall be done or foreborne by one or both - also a writing in which the terms of a bargain are included - an agreement enforceable by law - to agree upon, to establish by agreement - to undertake mutually or enter upon - to become involved in - to draw the parts together - collect - concentrate' *(Shorter Oxford Dictionary).*

The contract can be seen as a method of neutralizing threats explicit or implicit toward the group leader by members of the group. Fagan in Tasks of the Therapist (Fagan and Shepherd, 1970) says:

'One of the most effective ways of neutralizing such threats is to make a clear contract initially. Szasz informs patients that they will need to make arrangements with someone else if they require hospitalisation: Goulding requires signed contracts from potentially suicidal patients in which they agree without reservation to make no suicide attempts while they are seeing him.'

Both the therapists quoted by Fagan were using the concept of a contract in individual therapy as a means of control and of eliminating from the situation factors which might possibly have nullified treatment. The same application may well be used with groups. In the same book *Gestalt Therapy Now* Ennis and Mitchell in an article on Staff Training for a Day-care Centre are writing about the arrival of a consultant at the day-care centre:

'On the day of our first session, all of us were excited and/or scared. Our consultant began by making a "contract" with each of us for the first meeting. These contracts involved our stating one thing that we wanted from that meeting for ourselves (for example, better understanding of a co-worker, the opportunity to deal with unresolved conflicts and/or unexpressed feelings) and his agreeing to help us get it. "Getting something for ourselves" remained the theme of our first six sessions. We now had a time when we could explore the feelings that made us uncomfortable, clarify our communications, and risk new ways of relating. Our consultant gave us his support and knowledge as we struggled to express our anger, hurt, tenderness, and love. He also had the courage to shatter our fantasies and to confront us with our manipulations and projections. We discovered that growth is sometimes painful, sometimes joyful, and always rewarding.'

Rose differentiates between a 'treatment' contract and a 'behavioural' contract as follows: 'The treatment contract involves a statement of the general responsibilities of members and therapist over an extended period of time. The behavioural contract is a formal statement of a specific set of agreements - what the client is expected to do over a given period of time for a given reward' (1972).

Rose goes on to indicate that clear knowledge about treatment and agreement to be involved in treatment are positively correlated with success. He links this to the fact that knowing what is to be learnt and the process of learning increase the possibility of success: 'Since all therapies manipulate, a therapeutic approach in which the client knows about and agrees

to that manipulation is more acceptable to the individual and
society at large' (1972). Anxiety is reduced when people know
about the situations in which they will be involved and drop-out
rates are reduced.

Treatment Contract

Rose defines a 'preliminary' contract and a 'primary' contract,
the former implying an agreement to survey what is being offered
without any explicit commitment by the client that he will
accept involvement. In other words, this is clearly a pre-sale
demonstration, a sampling process which allows the prospective
clients to see, to talk about, and to acquaint themselves with
what is being offered. This period ends when the client having
satisfied himself about the situation either decides this is not for
him and opts out, or moves on to establish a stronger
commitment - a primary contract. The preliminary contract is an
extended effort to clear expectations and may be used to draw
prospective clients closer to the point where they are ready to
be committed to the treatment process.

The primary contract is an agreement to move toward a
change of behaviour in exchange for help and the services of the
therapist and his resources. This contract is open to renegotiation
as the client becomes more committed, or sees new prospects
are available. Churchill (1965) defines a 'secondary' contract in
which a client is prepared not only to work on his own behaviour,
with which he has had some success, but also to help his peers
with their problems.

The extract from 'A Behavioural Approach to the Group
Treatment of Parents' (1969) by Rose given below clearly outlines
the assessment and goal-setting procedures used in one particular
instance. By implication the author of the article is saying that
the parents are encouraged to formulate a 'baseline' from
which to evaluate any changes in their childrens' behaviour and
that the techniques which they learn are part of an agreed
process between parent and therapist - the latter offering his
knowledge and skill, the parent offering co-operative
participation:

Assessment

'One of the major difficulties of parents who come to an agency is the inadequacy or inappropriateness of their child management procedures − the skills necessary to cope with their children's behavior. The purpose of behavioral group treatment is to increase their repertoire of procedures and to teach them the appropriate conditions under which these techniques should be applied.

Before the parent can be taught these skills, it is necessary to determine the child's presenting behavioral problem. The parent learns to state the problem in terms of observable behaviors that occur or fail to occur in specific situations. He is also shown ways of estimating (or counting) how often they take place, since it is the frequency that is most often changed. Because most parents are not accustomed to speaking in specific terms about behaviour and many lack observational skills that are prerequisite to any description or counting, in most groups considerable time is given to training them to do so.

This training involves observing social situations, counting specific behaviors, charting these behaviors, and reporting the results to the group. In order to increase the probability of success, the parents first observe and count behaviors with which they are not especially concerned, e.g. the number of times the child leaves and enters the room, the context and number of situations in which he smiles or laughs. As they gain skill in observation, they note the frequency of the behaviors, with which they are concerned, e.g. complaining, temper-tantrums, soiling, teasing a sibling, being a traunt. At this point a baseline - an estimate of the frequency of the behavioral problem prior to any endeavor at change - is established.

The baseline makes it possible to evaluate the degree of the child's behavioral changes as treatment progresses. However, in the experience described in this paper, several difficulties arose that frequently made it necessary to rely on indefinite estimates or to forego a baseline completely. Some of these problems were the parents' different levels of comprehension, their inadequate training, "forgetting," and lack of co-operation by one of the spouses.

There is considerable evidence to support the contention that the events that follow a given behavior or the immediate consequences of that behavior have a strong influence on subsequent performances of it. This is one of the basic precepts of learning theory and it forms the foundation for many forms of intervention. For this reason, parents are taught to observe and describe the immediate results of all their child's behaviors with which they are concerned. One set of consequences over which the parents have the most control are their own reactions - emotional, verbal, and motor. Once the parents are able to describe their responses, a major part of the treatment involves assessing them and training the parents in new or more appropriate ones.

In order to determine which behaviors should be modified, the worker also reviews the long-range consequences of each behavioral problem with the parents. In this process, many parents discover that the ultimate effects of one set of behaviors are relatively unimportant or, because of the consequences of previously unconsidered behaviors, they warrant immediate attention.

The following example is an excerpt from a group meeting in which some of the aspects of assessment are dominant.

"Mrs. M. complained that her 11-year-old daughter had frequent temper tantrums. The members inquired about the conditions that led to them. Mrs. M., after reflecting a moment, indicated that her daughter responded this way whenever the mother said "no" or she became frustrated in any way. When asked what happened when she had these tantrums, Mrs. M. said she usually gave her daughter exactly what she wanted in order to quiet her down. Mrs. W. asked what might eventually happen if this habit were to persist. Throwing up her hands, Mrs. M. replied that it would drive the whole family out of their minds and probably her teacher and friends, too."

The members then suggested to Mrs. M. that she was maintaining the behavior she wanted to eliminate by rewarding her daughter after the temporary tantrum. This implied the change procedures to be used: Mrs. M. would have to find some alternative response to the temper tantrum, such as ignoring her, walking away, using calm verbal expression, and/or isolating her until the tantrum wore off.

Goal-Setting

After assessing the problem, each set of parents is helped by other parents to establish a goal of the desired frequency or intensity of behaviour they would like to see their children achieve. The goals are formulated along the same dimension as those in relation to the presenting behavior or the conditions under which a behavior is appropriate. As is true of initial behavioral problems, the criteria of specificity and the description of the impinging conditions are essential in the statement of goals. The kind of goals dealt with include increasing the frequency of studying to one hour an evening, eliminating temper tantrums, reducing the frequency of fighting with a sibling to twice a week, learning new ways of responding to external stress or limitations, discriminating between situations in which loud, raucous play is appropriate or inappropriate, and increasing the frequency of coming home on time to every evening.

The worker also evolves with each parent or set of parents the goal each parent expects to achieve for himself by the end of treatment. Many parents are initially hesitant to look at ways in which they themselves must change in order to establish the desired changes in their children and, as a result, prefer to focus solely on the changes in the child. The worker may postpone encouraging the parent to make explicit the goal of his own behavioral change in the first phase of treatment. However, the need for parental changes usually becomes obvious as soon as the children's behaviors are evaluated.

Examples of goals for parental change include ignoring temper tantrums and providing attention for more desirable behaviors, establishing rules and routines and ways of maintaining them, giving rewards in a consistent rather than haphazard manner, and learning and practising the forms of manifesting interest in the child's school and recreational activities.

The process of assessment and goal-setting begins in an

intake interview and is continued in the group. Dealing with these tasks in the group provides each parent with an opportunity to help others specify their problems and impinging conditions and to observe on repeated occasions the relation of these conditions to the problem. The group members gradually take over from the worker the responsibility of determining whether the problem and goal are sufficiently specific and the conditions adequately described. By analyzing and dealing with problems other than their own they increase their problem-solving skills in general and are better able to cope with new problems that may arise after the group terminates' (1969: 22-4).

Behavioural Contract

Rose quotes the form of this contract from Krumboltz and Thoresen as an:

agreement between two or more persons specifying what each person will do for a stated period of time. It takes the form, I'll do . . . for you, in exchange for your doing . . . for me. A time limit is usually stated or implied. The contract is re-negotiable whenever either of the parties to it thinks the terms of the contract are unfair to him (1969).

Behavioural contracts can be made with a group i.e. negotiated with the group as a whole, rather than with an individual. Rose emphasizes that client participation is increased by contract negotiation.

Behavioural Assignments

These are contracts for work to be done between meetings which should be clearly specific, and alternatives to cover unforeseen eventualities are usually included. Successful completion of the assignment should be rewarded as soon as possible afterwards.

Enough has been said to demonstrate the basic concept of contract. Clearly the effort to involve clients, group members, patients, in deciding what they want out of the group situation is one which is not only ethically sound but also effective. In essence, the establishment of a real contract which is renegotiable puts into the hands of the group member or the group as a whole the ability to control the degree of involvement which normally gets lost when a paternalistic treatment agency is believed to possess unlimited power.

Contracts may be verbal or written, but always they should provide clear evidence to the group members that what they are entering upon will be controlled by their wishes and not by the dictates of some all-powerful person. There are, however, several words of warning required. Groups are used in all kinds of situations and are in no way divorced from the milieu in which they are held. They are interdependent in the sense that members of one group exist in other groups and bring in experience gained elsewhere; they also take out experience gained in that group to the others to which they belong. The kind of contract which can be established must take cognizance of this fact and also of the realistic limitations of the environment in which the group exists.

A contract cannot therefore be made which goes against what is possible. In a very short space of time it will be seen to be unrealistic and the group will feel cheated. The whole concept of contract is one of sharing and understanding and to create a contract in which members accept in good faith boundaries of control which are not consonant with what is actually possible will undoubtedly bring into question the motives of the group leader who was inconsiderate enough or dishonest enough to allow such a thing to occur, or at least to keep quiet about it.

Like all groupwork tools, contract obviously has to be used with discretion. Its great advantage is that it is a demonstrably caring instrument. Words used to describe intentions can so easily be misinterpreted, or even not heard. Actions, behaviour, are less susceptible to conscious control, and in contrast with words, behaviour is most often seen to represent the truer state of affairs. Contract is a piece of behaviour on the part of the group leader which carries a much greater chance of being interpreted by group members as a genuine democratic move than any amount of statements about the democracy of the group. Of course, if contract is used by the group leader as a gimmick in order to win the consent of group members to particular moves of his devising, then this piece of bogus behaviour will eventually destroy such a contract.

REFERENCES

Churchill, S. (1965) Social Groupwork: A Diagnostic Tool in Child Guidance: *Am. J. Orthopsychiatry* 35 (3): 581-8.

Ennis K. and Mitchell, S. Staff Training for a Day Centre. In J. Fagan and I. L. Shepherd (eds.) Harmondsworth: Penguin Books 1972 *Gestalt Therapy Now.*

Fagan, J. (1972) The Tasks of the Therapists. In J. Fagan and I.L. Shepherd (eds.) *Gestalt Therapy Now.* Harmondsworth: Penguin.

Hartford, M. E. (1971) *Groups in Social Work.* N.Y.:Columbia U.P.

Krumboltz, J. D. and Thorsen, C. E. (eds.) (1969) *Behavioural Counselling: Cases and Techniques.* N.Y.: Holt, Rinehart & Winston.

Rose, S. D. (1972) *Treating Children in Groups.* London: Jossey-Bass.

Rose, S. D. (July 1969) A Behavioural Approach to the Group Treatment of Parents. *Social Work 14* (3).

4

Leaders, co-leaders and resource persons

Democratic societies seem to be fascinated by the ways in which groups of people may be led, by the qualities of leadership, and by the kinds of situation from which leaders arise. Skynner writing about family therapy indicates that he sees child development as a 'series of challenges to master group situations of increasing complexity'. He sees the development process as a preparation for leadership, by a process of adaptation to the authority of others, culminating in the assumption of a leadership role: 'Adolescence finally brings pressures, both internal and external, thrusting the individual out of the family to find his main support among his peers, to mate and begin the process again, as leader this time of a new family group' (1969: 81-106).

Viewed in this way, leadership problems are a fundamental part of human existence, and the ways in which individuals have learned to tackle such problems form much of the substance of interaction in groups.

Concepts of leadership have gone through several stages, starting with the premise that leadership required a combination of personality traits which were distinguishable from those possessed by followers, through situational factors which highlighted the assets of a given person at a given time, to a multi-dimensional approach which is also eclectic. Out of this has come an interest in leadership acts rather than in long-term dominance. Bids for leadership are made by most individuals in a small group as a result of the way they perceive the group's behaviour and their own reactions at any moment in the existence of the group.

This kind of knowledge about group leadership is valuable for the group worker mainly because his role needs to be clearly defined and his relationship to the group made explicit for the group to be able to work with him. Bion (1961) has exposed the way in which groups expect and demand a leadership function from a group worker and he has also demonstrated the anxieties which a refusal to accept this role creates.

Most group workers when starting with a group are concerned not so much with the theoretical aspects of leadership, but with the practical problems of exercising such a role and being able to assess how their leadership efforts can be made more effective. Primarily, this arises because group workers, with the exception of family therapists, work with 'created' groups and the process of selection tends to put the group worker into the position of being the only person in the group with a prior relationship with every other member. This role was designated by Redl (1942) as that of 'Central Person' and creates not only a position for the group worker to occupy, but necessarily a series of expectations of how he will function in it.

Much of the writing about leadership tends to be concerned with the way leaders arise in group situations, exercise the functions of planning, decision-making or co-ordinating, and the way acts of leadership contribute to group performance. This kind of material is useful for the group worker in that it highlights the sources of opposition and challenge to his own attempts at leadership during the period of the group's life when such leadership is either desirable, necessary, or viable. Traditionally leadership has been conceived of as the exercise of power, a factor which has not responded very well to analysis but which is customarily seen as the ability to influence intentionally the behaviour of others.

Task Leaders and Emotional Leaders

Expressing concern about the expectations of the members of a group, Verba (1967) discusses the effect this has on what he calls 'emergent' leaders as opposed to 'legitimate' leaders. It becomes obvious that the characteristics which are essential in achieving leadership are not necessarily consonant with those characteristics which are needed to maintain a leadership role.

The group worker may well conceive of his role as being legitimate in the sense that the expectations of his group will tend to define his role in this way. It is possible that he may combine the roles of task and emotional leader, but it seems more likely that as such roles are usually accepted by different people in a group, he may opt for one only, the other being supplied by an emergent leader from the group. Verba points out that sharing the roles in this way reduces conflict and serves to limit the confounding of expectations. It also appears to cause a high level of interaction between the two leaders.

As group workers do not always operate solo, particularly in residential settings where sharing their group leadership with colleagues is common, the problems of sharing leadership are of considerable interest.

There are two main categories of leadership functions. Those required to meet the needs at the task level and those required to meet the needs at the group maintenance level:

'1) Task functions - these leadership functions are to facilitate and to co-ordinate group effort in the selection or definition of a common problem and in the solution of that problem. They include:

Initiating - the proposing of tasks or goals, defining the group problem, suggesting a procedure, or ideas for solving a problem.

Information or opinion-seeking - requesting facts, seeking relevant information about a group concern, asking for suggestions and ideas.

Information or opinion-giving - offering facts, providing relevant information about group concerns, stating a belief, giving suggestions or ideas.

Clarifying or elaborating - interpreting or reflecting ideas and suggestions, clearing confusions, indicating alternatives and issues before the group, giving examples.

Summarising - pulling together related ideas, restating suggestions after the group has discussed them, offering a decision or conclusion for the group to accept or reject.

Consensus testing - sending up trial balloons to see if the group is nearing a conclusion, checking with the group to see how much agreement has been reached.

2) Maintenance functions - functions in this category describe leadership activities necessary to alter or maintain the way in which members of the group work together, developing loyalty to one another and to the group as a whole.

Encouraging - being friendly, warm, and responsive to others and to their contributions, showing regard for others by giving them an opportunity for recognition.

Expressing group feelings - sensing feelings, moods, relationships within the group, sharing feelings with other members.

Harmonising - attempting to reconcile disagreements, reducing tension by pouring oil on troubled waters, getting people to explore their differences.

Compromising - when one's own idea or status is involved in a conflict, offering to compromise one's own position, admitting error, disciplining oneself to maintain group cohesion.

Gate-keeping - attempting to keep communication channels open, facilitating the participation of others, suggesting procedures for the discussion of group problems.

Setting standards - expressing standards for the group to achieve, applying standards and evaluating group functioning and production.' (Lippitt and Seashore)

Leadership Effectiveness

Some studies are concerned to show that the task leader and the emotional leader are not necessarily exclusive kinds of leadership, but that each is more effective in certain situations than the other. Thus the simple statement is made that 'directive, managerial, active leaders perform best under conditions which provide them with either considerable or with relatively little effective power. Permissive, considerate, non-directive leaders perform best in group situations intermediate in the degree of effective power which the leader has at his disposal' (Backman and Secord, 1966).

Clearly the first leader is task-oriented; he holds the members to the job in hand constantly reminding them of their essential purpose. Equally clearly the second leader is the affective leader who is concerned with the smoothing of relationships within the group. So whereas the sharing of leadership has been mentioned previously, Fiedler is concerned to show that a leader of either of these types will be more effective if the situation in which he exercises his leadership is of a particular nature.

For the group worker this is a matter not so much of effectiveness, though this is important enough, but a question of leadership style. In essence this implies a knowledge on the part of the group worker of his own ability and the dominant feature of his leadership acts. Added to this must be the ability to recognize the degree of power he possesses or perhaps more accurately the degree of power which he can be seen by the group members to possess.

Given the fact that a group worker wishes to act as a leader then Fiedler's model offers the possibility of predicting the level of success such a leadership bid would achieve. Obviously there is always the possibility that although a given worker's leadership style may lie in one direction, he may have the ability to assume a leadership role in the other style if he becomes aware that the situation demands it.

Fiedler is also concerned with the concept of power which is traditionally associated with leadership. Designated leaders obviously possess power in that they are supported by the authority that appointed them. But as Fiedler's model depends upon recognizing the degree of power possessed by the leader it would be as well to point out that power is seen to reside in people for a variety of reasons and any group worker would be well advised to be aware of these sources in any attempt to assess his own power vis-a-vis his group.

French and Raven (1959) listed five sources of social power which may be summarized as follows:

'1) Reward power - perceived as able to reward behaviour
2) Coercive power - perceived as able to punish behaviour

3) Legitimate power - perceived as granted by authority
4) Expert power - perceived as possessing knowledge and expertise useful to the group
5) Referent power - perceived as being a person with whom members wish to identify.'

All leadership roles possess some of these factors, some possess all, but in any case the perceived strength of the power is equally relevant.

Figure 3 *Leadership*

Basis		*Basis*	
Appointed	Power	Group	Power essentially
Formal	essentially	Process	personal
	legitimate	Informal	

designated leader (External) imposed from outside group may not be a member usually directly connected to outside authority structure stays in power for a given term does not depend upon consensus

natural leader (Internal) arises within the group is always a member derives power from the group's agreement to his position may be deposed when usefulness is over depends on concensus may become fixed due to inertia

when
Group
Structure

is greater:
less dispute over
problems

is less:
more dispute over problems
no definition of situation
may create anxiety
leader then becomes person who
can reduce tension and define
problems

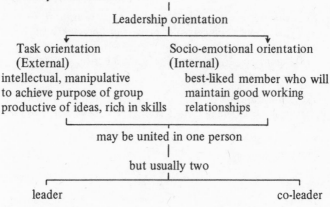

Leadership orientation

Task orientation (External)	Socio-emotional orientation (Internal)
intellectual, manipulative to achieve purpose of group productive of ideas, rich in skills	best-liked member who will maintain good working relationships

may be united in one person

but usually two

leader   co-leader

Power is given by people who perceive others to possess the ability to:

1) Reward
2) Punish

or as having:

3) Special abilities
4) Legitimate power (appointed by higher authority)
5) Referent power (charisma)

     Culture lays down the traditional ways in which this perception takes place

Leader = individual who influences the group most consistently over a more or less prolonged period and creates the expectation that he will exert influence.

Central Person

The idea of the 'Central Person' is a very interesting one for group workers in that it is concerned with a form of leadership based on common emotional responses to one person. It has already been noted that this concept originated with Redl in his observations in school settings.

Heap (1966) shows that the very nature of the professional group worker's situation, coupled with the needs and expectations of the client/members of the group, creates a common relationship of all the members to the group worker. Here is exactly the kind of leadership situation which Bion describes and, in his work with groups, refused to accept, in order that the group members shall be forced to come to terms with their expectations of leadership.

Heap on the other hand states that this situation is real and can be accepted because it is a way into the process of creating a working group. This implies that the leadership role, based upon being a 'Central Person', is distinctly appropriate to certain kinds of groups and is inevitably appropriate to their beginning stages when the need of a central, focal point is great. Thus groups which are created for a specific purpose by the person who is going to act as group worker already have this kind of common relational factor and to frustrate it is either pointless or demanding a great deal, not only of skill but of certainty of the purpose and ability of the group.

As the group grows together the relationship of the members to each other becomes stronger and their relationship to the group worker must therefore be modified. In a group of strangers the group worker has been the focal point not only because of his assumed professional skills, but also because he knew everyone before they met as a group. After a period of time all the members have gained 'shared experience and any leadership function which the group worker exercises must now depend upon the group's perception of his professional skills. So Heap stresses the necessity of being aware of the changing and developing needs of a group established in this way and of the need to change the style of leadership in accord.

Maintenance of Leadership

If, as has already been argued, leadership depends not only on the personality of the leader, but also upon the situation present at the time, then some investigation of the kinds of situational factors involved should be rewarding. Bell and French (1950) set out to measure the way in which individuals maintained their leadership function when faced with groups of different individuals. Their findings are interesting in that they point to only a very small influence toward consistency of leadership performance being constantly present. This would tend to indicate that in the kind of small group used in the experiment, the personality of the leader is of paramount importance and the situation is a contributory, rather than a causative, factor in the appearance of leaders.

This finding should of course be regarded with some degree of caution in view of the peculiar nature of the groups used and the 'one-off' nature of each event. The authors indicate their awareness of this in their concluding remarks. But there is also the possibility of a degree of sophistication of those taking part by virtue of the repetitive nature of the experiment. However when all these factors are taken into consideration there is some need to be wary of the current emphasis on the situational factor as the authors' stress in their last sentence. From the point of view of those working with groups this kind of evidence tends to stress the personality factors of leaders; and to increase the necessity of discovering a leadership style compatible both with using the potential of the group worker in the most effective way, and also with fulfilling the aims of the group.

Cartwright and Zander (1960) writing about leadership acts indicate that in order for a group member to initiate such an act he must:

a) be aware that a given function is needed, and

b) feel that he is able to perform it, has enough skill to do so, and that it is safe to attempt it.

For the group worker in the position of being group leader, i.e. a designated leader, these two factors remain indispensable if he is to function effectively.

In an article called 'Leaders for Laboratory Training: selected guidelines for group trainers utilising the laboratory method', G.L. Lippitt and L.E. This identify six roles which the group leader has to perform. These are as follows:

1) initiator of diagnostic training concepts

2) diagnostic observer at appropriate time and level

3) innovator of learning experience

4) standards protector

5) initiator of selected group standards for learning

6) group member function

They go on to outline some special problems and pitfalls and these are listed as follows:

1) leader becomes too directive

2) leader and group become too clinical

3) leader becomes too personally involved in the group

4) the group is used in an inappropriate way

5) mistaking frustration and floundering for learning

The following is an edited version of the final paragraphs of this article which is headed 'Comments on Trainer Intervention':

The group leader's role in group work frequently involves him directly in the learning experience. He may be part of a 'here and now' experience, involved in a role-play, a member of a discussion or a diagnostic session, leader of a case study or group exercise, or an observer of the group and its processes.

At such times, the trainer frequently is faced with the question 'Should I intervene in the group discussion, or activity, or should I let the group find its own way?'. There are several guidelines which will assist the group worker in making decisions about interventions:

1) Intervention by the worker has as its purpose, for the most part, the learning of the group about its processes.

2) Worker interventions may be helpful to both the individual and the group in giving support to make possible the exposure of behaviour for analysis.

3) Intervention by the worker in encouraging the use of feedback amongst the members of the group, for both individual and group learning.

4) Worker intervention may be necessary if, in the professional judgement of the worker, a particular individual or subgroup is being over-threatened by the analysis of the group. Individuals and groups vary very widely in their ability to tolerate such feedback and perception.

5) As the group takes over the observer function, the interventions of the worker can become less frequent and at a different level from the observations being made by the group.

6) Worker interventions may be of a procedural nature to maximize learning within the group experience.

7) Near the end of the group work experience there is frequently an expectancy on the part of the group members not only to share their feelings about one another and the ways they have seen one another, but also for the worker to share with the group his feelings and observation about the group's growth, learning, and effectiveness. At this stage in the group's experience, such sharing is a legitimate aspect of the intervention and member role responsibility of the worker.

These thoughts about the role of group worker interventions are suggestive of their relationship to the learning process;

although interventions are basically conditioned by the goals of the group work process they are constantly affected by the situation, time, and member and worker needs. It is also likely that worker intervention will be affected by the group's concept of the worker's role as experienced by the group and redefined at various points in the life of the group.

A leader often wants to know: 'How can I get members to participate more fully in my group?', 'What makes an effective group?', 'How can I keep group discussion on the track?', 'What causes cliques to form and how can they be handled?', 'Why do members so often have trouble understanding one another?', 'How can a group examine its own functioning?', 'When is group decision-making more practical than individual decision-making?'. The ability of a group to function properly is not necessarily dependent upon the leader. No group can become fully productive until its members are willing to assume responsibility for the way the group acts. Any group can benefit from a skilled leader, but to get creative group thinking, group decisions, and group action, research evidence indicates that many different roles are required. The effective leader must realize, and help the members to realize, that contributing to the total task of leadership is a responsibility of each member.

Leader behaviour in a group can range from almost complete control of the decision-making by the leader to almost complete control by the group, with the leader contributing his resources just like any other group member. A leader can assume most of the functions required to provide leadership for the group, or these functions can become the responsibility of the members as well.

Co-Leaders and Resource Persons

Many recorded groups have been set up with two or more practitioners involved in the leadership role. It may well be that there is a great deal of comfort to be gained from entering into a leadership role with a partner. There is the consideration of support, of two sets of ideas and observations, and possibly the fact that two people set 'against' several others are likely to be much more seriously regarded than one person in such a situation. The supportive role of the co-leader is probably a very valuable one for group leaders who are aware of the difficulties and yet have possibly no other method of help available to them in running their groups.

The main advantages of employing a co-leader may be listed as follows:
1) support
2) sharing
3) splitting leader roles
4) feedback on each other's leadership performance
5) role model of co-operative leadership.

Support has already been covered, and sharing is somewhat similar. The latter involves taking turns in bearing the responsibility of guiding the group, of feeding in observations, ideas, information, etc., thus reducing the amount of stress placed upon either leader.

The great advantage of co-leadership lies in being able to split leadership functions and styles. One leader can then become oriented towards maintaining harmonious relationships and the other towards getting on with the job. Such splitting can alternate so that each leader is able to perform either functional role within the group.

Another large advantage in this co-operative leadership performance is the fact that it frees one leader to concentrate on observing. This is an activity which is beneficial from at least two points of view. First, freed from worry about being in the leadership role, the co-leader can take time to observe closely the responses and interaction in the group, thereby coming to a greater appreciation and understanding of that group and all others. Second, he is able to use this enhanced understanding for the benefit of the group on the basis that the bystander sees more of the game than the players.

Feedback from the situation must also accrue to each of the leaders about how each sees the other's performance. The leadership role can cut off the occupant of it from a great deal of feedback about his leadership behaviour. He can become so absorbed in the role that he misses the clues which are offered about how he is being received. His 'blind spots' can easily be seen by a co-leader in the observer role and his own personal growth thereby assured.

Finally, the co-leadership function offers an example of

co-operative and complementary function which may well form a very important part of the learning of the group members, especially if the inability to work co-operatively is part of a common problem.

The co-leader's role is marked by his ability to look objectively at the group process. The feedback from this observation enables the group to move forward. The co-leader may use an evaluative questionnaire like the one given here for this purpose:

Table 4 Co-Leader's Questionnaire for Evaluating Group Process

Atmosphere:
Warm, friendly, informal?
Is there good group morale?
Are members sensitive to the feelings of others?

Tempo:
Too slow?
Too hurried?

Interest Level:
High? medium? low?
Are many people bored?
Are there signs of fatigue?
Are people really interested in the topic under discussion?

Content:
Is discussion specific and practical, or theoretical?

Progress:
Is the problem clearly understood?
Is there decision on possible steps to be taken in solving the problem?
Are major points jotted down to assist the group in crystallizing its thinking?

Participation:
Is discussion monopolized by a few people?
Do some people attempt to dominate?
Are there some persons who never say anything?

Does any member of the group set himself up as an expert and try to answer all questions?

Is there merely a series of speeches?

Do persons communicate effectively?

Are contributions brief and to the point?

Is there an honest effort to understand each others' point of view?

Are needed roles assumed by members, such as clarifier, summarizer, encourager, humourist, initiator, realist?

He helps by pointing out ways in which the group process could be improved and by indicating the important features which have already occurred. Briefly he has the responsibility of discovering why the group behaves as it does and of offering ways of improving it.

One of the main problems of effective co-leadership is in finding two people who can Box and Cox effectively. Neither must take advantage of the other, neither must shirk his responsibilities. The relationship betwen co-leaders needs to be founded upon mutual trust and understanding and certain simple precautions may be taken to ensure the maximization of these bases:

1) Planning - part of the preparation for such a group should involve prospective co-leaders in a sharing of ideas and attitudes, of experience and theoretical orientations, and of preparing for the roles they intend to play and the cues to be given for changes to take place. Cues have in no sense to be covert, and should become part of the total group learning about leadership processes.

2) Constant consultation - before and after each group, feedback on behavioural patterns should accompany the planning and analysis. Any points of conflict need to be confronted and resolved. Techniques grow from such meetings.

3) Shared experience — as a group becomes aware of its existence *qua* group by sharing a considerable amount of relevant experience, so co-leaders become more aware of the way they work together as they share leadership experiences.

Resource persons

Within any group there will be people who possess resources, abilities, knowledge, skill, which is of value to the group at certain times in its existence. In this sense everyone in the group is a resource person in that he contributes what he has to the group's existence. But certain people have resources not widely distributed. When these resources are required these people become of special value to the group, are invested with 'specialist' power, and may assume a temporary leadership role: good leadership and effective group organization include a knowledge of all the resources available for use.

A second kind of resource person is the one who is not a member of the group which wishes to use his special skill. In this case he is brought in as a consultant or special assistant to help the group to function. This facilitative role carries with it certain privileges in that the occupant is usually accorded certain of the statuses attached to leadership, but is not often actually included in the group. When his functions are no longer needed his privileges are frequently rescinded or changed, usually in the form of decreasing his power.

REFERENCES

Bell, G. B. and French, R. L. (1950) Consistency of Individual Leadership Positions in Small Groups. *Journal of Abnormal and Social Psychology* **45**: 764-7.

Bion, W. R. (1961) *Experience in Groups.* London: Tavistock Publications.

Fiedler, F. (1965). The Contingency Model. In Harold Proshansky and B. Seidenberg (eds.) *A Theory of Leadership Effectiveness in Basic Studies in Social Psychology.* New York: Holt, Rinehart, and Winston.

French, J.R.P. and B. Ravens (1959). The Bases of Social Power. In Dorwin Cartwright (ed.) *Studies in Social Power.* Ann Arbor: Michigan Inst. for Soc. Research.

Heap, K. (1966). The Groupworker as Central Person, *Case Conference* **12** (7): 20-9.

Lippett, G.L. and Seashore, E.W. The Leader Looks at Group Effectiveness in *Looking into Leadership* (pamphlet).

Lippitt, G.L. and This, L.E. (1970). Leaders for Laboratory Training. In Robert T. Golembiewski and Arthur Blumberg (eds.) *Sensitivity Training and the Laboratory Approach.* Ill., U.S.A.:

F. E. Peacock.

Redl, F. (1942) Group Emotion and Leadership. *Psychiatry* **5** (4).

Skynner, A.C. (1969) A Group Analytic Approach to Conjoint Family Therapy. *J. of Child Psychol. and Allied Disciplines* **10.**

Verba, S. (1961). Leadership: Affective and Instrumental. In *Small Groups and Political Behaviour.* Princeton, N.J.: Princeton Univ. Press.

5

Size of groups

A fact which tends to emerge more clearly than most from the welter of material on groups is that each factor which is isolated for examination, e.g. size or membership or leadership, etc., is an integral part of each group. Separation therefore creates an analogous situation to an attempt to understand the individual organs of a body after they have been removed from it. The whole aspect of function which depends upon being part of a living organism and on receiving and transmitting information, action impulses, etc., tends to disappear.

This fact has great value for people who work with groups because alteration to any one of the factors like size, or membership of a given group, creates change to a greater or lesser degree in every other factor. Many of these changes are known and have been examined; they can therefore be used consciously to achieve recognized ends. It must become obvious that any intervention other than that based upon some such foreknowledge as this is either based on intuition or is working in the dark.

Size is a factor which has come in for a fair amount of investigation basically because man has always recognized that beyond a certain number for a given job, there will be too many people who may be either underemployed or a great hindrance to those who are able to function. The converse is also easily recognized, i.e. where there are too few people they may be either unable to perform a task at all, or vastly overworked.

The kind of task tends to dictate the size of the group needed to perform it; alternatively where group size is either too great or too small for the avowed task, then it is more than likely that the task may undergo some form of modification. Industry provides many examples of this, from short-time workings to redundancy, from underemployment and feather-bedding to overwork.

Quite a great deal of group research has been devoted to the differences, usually in individual performance, between an individual working by himself and in a group. However, many of the findings are irrelevant to group workers, except in so far as they show how group pressures can enforce a level of conformity on the individual even when he is not much committed to the group with which he is working, or perhaps to show how adverse group pressures may be resisted and overcome.

McGrath and Altman (1966), after commenting on the unsystematic nature of much of the research on group size, point out that the following apparently consistent relationships emerge. Relatively small group size is likely to be accompanied by the following:
1) less perceived need for guidance and for a definite leader
2) fewer expressed ideas and less change in attitudes or other responses by members
3) less frequent perceptions of the leader as exhibiting co-ordinating behaviour, clarifying rules, or wisely delegating authority
4) greater perception of group task success.

Other factors which may concern the group worker relating to the size of group may well be physical and material. Thus in a 'talk' group, if every member is to be in contact with every other member, then close visual contact is essential. Human vision being as restricted as it is this tends to dictate a small number of people usually in a circular arrangement for maximum visual contact. Material conditions may be simply the amount of space available in the possible venue.

As would be expected, group size can be shown to influence

the effectiveness of a group: 'group cohesiveness and member
satisfaction tend to be greater in small groups; there is evidence
that larger groups inhibit participation of some members; style
of leadership varies with group size; the relationship between
group size and effectiveness is complex and variable'.

(Krech, Crutchfield and Ballachey, 1962: 470).

In his research on size as a factor in the success of discussion
groups, Schellenberg found that group size was correlated with
student satisfaction. 'Students claim greater satisfaction in the
smaller groups. Instructors are more inclined than students to
show satisfaction with larger groups. There was limited evidence
that smaller groups showed slightly higher academic achievement
than did large groups' (1959).

This may be taken as a clear indication that if group size is
related to satisfaction then size must also be related to the
percieved purpose of the group and the degree of its achievement.
Instructors and students would surely have significantly different
perceived purposes, the former relating to maximum effect
through minimum effort, and the latter relating to the satisfaction
of their individual need to learn.

Group Size and Interaction

Three of the important effects of group size on interaction are:
1) If there is a given period of time in which the group operates,
then the time available for each person to talk decreases with
increases in group size.
2) There are some unique associations with given sizes, e.g. a
group of two cannot form a majority except by agreeing.
3) The formation of subgroups is affected by group size.

Depending upon the function of a group and its purpose, it
should be possible to find an optimum size at which all necessary
processes have room to operate effectively.

A group which is too large for its purpose and organization
pushes certain members out to the periphery and denies them
access to the lines of communication and control. This creates a
situation favourable to the formation of dissident subgroups
which may become the focus of rebellion and of bids for power.

Where decisions have to be taken, then even-numbered groups
are traditionally held to be at a disadvantage since there is the

possibility of an even division on any given topic. Thus there is great support here for the idea that any group worker should be able to relate the size of his group to its purpose in order to ensure that the factor of size is positively functioning for the group rather than cluttering its progress or creating hazards...

'There are differences between persons as to the range of relationships they can encompass, based on prior experiences and factors of personality. It has been found that "increasing maturity of the personality associated with age permits effective participation in larger groups"... But, note that people may be retarded in their social development. Age does influence size, to some extent. Young children become overstimulated and confused in a group that seems large; they need to work out their problems in relationships with a few as they move toward efforts in co-operation. Latency age children usually need small groups to provide security as they work toward mastery of situations, but there are some cultural differences in this respect. Children from large, economically deprived families often are not ready for the intimacy of a very small group. These are examples of the need to determine size of group in terms of its purpose and the capacities of its members. There is no substitute for sound judgement in planning.' (Northen, 1970: 91-100).

Henderson and Leach recorded some of the problems they had encountered in setting up a club group for adolescents. Along with many other interesting facts of group process, this article contains some very apposite comments about the effect of size, not only on the purpose of the group, but also on its performance and the loyalty of the members. The article is quoted in full below:

'The "Thursday Club" is the name given by its members to a club/group for adolescents in the Tooting area of London. It was started by a group of child-care officers following the offer of the use of a well-appointed room at the premises of the Wandsworth Council for Community Relations. It was decided to start a group for teenagers partly to fill an apparent gap in local youth services and partly, as part of the Children's Department's preventive work, to offer some form of counselling service to young people who had no formal contact with the department, yet seemed likely to need help with such problems as family relationships, identity and authority.

A few youngsters known professionally to the workers (for example, school truants and the children from families in rent arrears) were invited to come and bring their friends. Numbers rapidly increased but there was no selection on the part of the workers. Those who came at first all lived in the same area, attended the same schools or worked together, and already knew each other to some extent. There were, however, various sub-groups, divided chiefly by age and sex. Some of the original workers subsequently dropped out, to be replaced by other interested CCOs and a solitary probation officer.

From the start, there was general agreement that there should be a non-authoritarian regime, to provide the members with an experience of adults different from the one to which they were felt to be accustomed. The aim was to counteract possible previous bad experiences with parents, teachers, police or employers through a relationship with an accepting adult. There was, however, considerable divergence of opinion about how best to achieve this aim. At one end there was the feeling that an attempt should be made to create a free-and-easy atmosphere, so that the members would feel able to drop in and out, with little real commitment. At the other extreme, a premium was placed on verbal communication between members and workers.

In the event, after a lengthy period of testing out, the members themselves imposed a working compromise in which they used the club both as a congenial background for social interaction amongst themselves, and at the same time as an opportunity for interaction, both verbal and otherwise, with the workers, according to their individual and collective needs. There were differing fantasies among the workers about what might happen. On the one hand, they visualised general lack of control, leading to damage to property or even "mob violence"; on the other hand, there were fears that the whole project would be ignored or rejected by the youngsters.

Non-authoritarian regime. In accordance with the agreed

general aim of establishing a non-authoritarian regime, the evening's "activity" was left to the members themselves. A record-player was provided, but it was left to them to bring records. Coffee could be made in the adjoining kitchen, but only if the members collected money and brought the necessary provisions. The only direct intervention by the workers was to convene most weeks a "meeting", at which difficulties, problems and perhaps complaints could be put to the assembled members for their comments, suggestions and opinions. On rare occasions, where it seemed especially appropriate, workers made comments interpreting the group's behaviour.

Three elements were built into the project from the beginning, designed to enable the workers to develop an awareness of what was going on within the group. First, after each meeting of the group, the workers held a brief discussion to share observations and experience, to try to make sense of what had happened during the evening. Secondly, a regular written record of all group meetings was kept. Thirdly, periodic consultation meetings of all workers were held to examine trends and discuss problems. A senior member of the Children's Department acted as independent consultant at these meetings.

Although this has been the over-all pattern, the life of the club has changed and developed, and can be seen as having passed through three phases. The first was characterized by great uncertainty amongst the workers and much testing-out behaviour from the members. The uncertainty of the workers had a number of sources. Difference of opinion about the best way of achieving the aim of the club led to doubts as to whether anything positive was being or could be achieved. Working at the club involved much time and effort, and workers wanted to be reassured that it was worthwhile. Another difficulty was the need to accept a relatively passive role, in contrast to a more active casework role.

Workers' fears and fantasies. A third difficulty was the workers' inexperience of working with each other. When a situation arose with which a particular worker had to deal, he had to cope not only with the problem itself, but also with his fears and fantasies concerning the possible reaction of colleagues to any course of action he might choose. Finally, there was some anxiety about possible damage to the premises. This was not an entirely idle fear, for in the early stages the carpet suffered the rigours of coffee and chewing-gum and the windows often seemed threatened. This anxiety made it even more difficult to work together, and at one point the consultant discerned a "first team" and "second team" of workers, differing in the degree of their enthusiasm and of their ability to cope with the anxiety.

The testing-out behaviour of the members took a number of forms. Often the furniture and fittings were tampered with, giving the impression that actual damage was imminent. Lights were turned on and off, cigarettes were stubbed out on the carpet, cups were broken. From time to time there were fights, and on one occasion a fire was started in the kitchen. This placed great stress on the workers, who were already experiencing conflict regarding their professional identities within the club.

All these doubts and conflicts were crystallised in the question of numbers which was the issue dominating the first phase. Up to 40 members used to crowd into one fairly small room, sometimes spilling over into the garden. New youngsters came every week, and there was little to suggest that this growth would cease. Workers felt unable to cope with larger numbers, partly out of anxiety that the acting-out behaviour and damage to premises might get out of hand, and partly from the conviction that positive results could only be achieved with a constant group of manageable proportions.

Accordingly, the workers agreed in one of the regular consultation meetings that membership should be limited to those who had already attended the club. This was put to the members at a club meeting. Several acknowledged the problem, and eventually the policy of limited membership was agreed.
However, it was an illusion to suppose that this was a genuinely democratic decision. In subsequent weeks there were several crises, when established members tried to bring friends who had not been before. The workers were forced to adopt the very authoritarian posture they had sought to avoid in order to enforce their decision and on two occasions there were

mass walk-outs by the members in protest, although they gradually returned during the evening.

Definite commitment. This phase was brought to an end by two meetings. The first was one of the workers' regular consultation meetings. These meetings had invariably been crisis meetings, involved agonised soul-searching as to whether there was any real point in the club's continued existence. However, it was finally agreed that it was time to make a definite commitment both individual and collective. It was agreed to give the club a definite experimental life of 12 months and the majority of workers committed themselves to working in the club for at least that period, although one or two withdrew at that stage. This gave the club a stability and the workers a unity of purpose which had previously been lacking.

The second meeting was a further club meeting, at which the question of numbers was again discussed. This time the workers began by frankly acknowledging the hostility to which their enforcement of the previous decision had given rise. The problem of numbers was then placed before the members who, after genuine discussion, came to the same decision as the one which had previously been imposed on them. This effectively resolved the problem because the workers no longer felt obliged to enforce the rule whereas the members were less inclined to break it, because it was now "their" rule.

The second major phase in the life of the club was one of consolidation. During this phase the workers developed the confidence and mutual trust to operate with colleagues in the club situation. This mutual trust arose partly from the shared experience of having faced together and to some extent overcome a difficult and challenging situation partly from the pooling of anxieties, doubts and, increasingly, hopes in the regular meetings with the consultant and partly from the decrease in the general level of anxiety.

In the club itself it was a fairly quiet period. Numbers remained fairly high (30+) but testing-out behaviour largely subsided, and club meetings centred on the collection of money each week to make coffee. The workers left this

problem to the members themselves, attempting to clarify but
not to direct the discussion. This period was also characterized
by some covert sexual behaviour. Groups of girls went out of
their way to provoke the boys and vice versa. At times this
provocation was also directed at workers of the opposite sex.
The club became more successful in a conventional sense.
There was ample evidence that a feeling of belonging, of group
solidarity had developed among the members. Plans for a
variety of different activities were put forward. The
atmosphere was generally relaxed, and there was no longer a
barrier between members and workers. This phase culminated
in an improvisation session, suggested and organised by the
members themselves, in which an episode from a well-known
TV series was improvised, with members interestingly filling
roles which seemed to be extensions of their real life
personalities.

Using social work help. The third phase has taken a rather
unexpected turn. Numbers have dwindled to a "hard core"
of about a dozen, a group of younger girls and a group of
older boys. Although the girls have been demanding of the
workers' attention, it is the boys, and one boy in particular,
who have dominated the club. This boy was one of the few
members to continue in attention-seeking during the second
period. However, throughout this third phase he and some of his
friends have been involved in a long drawn-out court appearance,
and he has come to use the workers in quite a different way,
a way which bears close resemblance to the workers' professional
counselling role. It was as though he had learned to get the
workers' attention and to use them in a more acceptable way.
It remains, of course, a group situation and peer-group
constraints still dictate reactions to some extent. But the club
seems by a process of self-selection to have reached the
situation where its remaining members are those who need
and have learned to accept professional social work help in
the context of an unstructured club/group situation. Partly
because of the smaller numbers and partly because of the more
familiar role that they were called upon to play, the workers'
anxiety diminished still further, and one worker who joined at
this stage perceived no anxiety in the situation at all.

Any account of an experiment such as the "Thursday Club" is of necessity selective. Throughout its existence different members have used different workers in different ways. Also it continues to change and develop, and its future is difficult to predict. Nevertheless, it is our belief that many of the members have been able to form meaningful relationships with accepting adults, to modify some of their attitudes towards authority, and to develop greater personal responsi responsibility. For the workers the club has proved a learning experience in coping with the problems of adolescence within a group, in working with colleagues in face-to-face situations and in developing mutual support to deal with anxiety. Certainly it has proved a worthwhile experiment in using social work techniques in an unaccustomed setting.'

(1971: 21-4)

Groups which occur in the natural state vary in size according to the age of the members and the social milieu in which they occur, e.g. casual work or leisure groups may have as few as two or three members whereas a gang of adolescents may have ten or more members. Generally speaking, when a group increases in size, according to Hare (1962):

1) members tend to become less satisfied;
2) the number of potential relationships between individuals and subgroups increases;
3) the stress on the leader to co-ordinate group activity increases;
4) the amount of time each member has to communicate with other members decreases;
5) an increased number of individuals will feel either threatened or inhibited;
6) the gap between the most frequent participator and others tends to become proportionately greater;
7) the resources of the group will increase - more members, more abilities to draw on, and so the group may be more efficient up to the point of diminishing returns;
8) the time for getting the job done is usually reduced but this may be achieved at the cost of lowered efficiency per individual member;
9) the range of available ideas is increased but the difficulty

of gaining agreement may also be increased;

10) Communication problems arise:

a) the need to cover greater numbers may mean that mechanical information dissemination has to be used

b) the group may be less sensitive to minority or differing viewpoints, and thus

c) more autocratic decisions will be taken.'

Thus the size of a group must clearly be related to its purpose and group workers should be aware not only that purposes may be more difficult to achieve if the number of group members is inappropriate but also that the group may well not function at all. The list given above has been considered in detail by some writers. Hoffman says:

'The disproportionate influence of the self confident member on the group's decision-making would seem to grow with increases in group size. As groups grow the distribution of participation among the members becomes severely skewed with one or two people doing the talking [see 6 above]. The larger the group the more inhibited the introverted people are, unless they have a strong stake in the outcome. In such cases those who are willing to speak will railroad their ideas through the meeting. Potential dissenters are often reluctant to voice their opinions for fear of being thought deviant' [see 5 above] (1965: 107).

Other factors influenced by an increase in the size of the group are given by Davis as follows:

'There are more persons for - acquiring ⎫ information related

processing ⎬ to the group's

recalling ⎭ task

- developing more complex patterns of interpersonal relationships

The group's potential productivity is affected in accordance with the Lorge - Solomon Model A -

If the probability of a solution for an individual is .25 then that for a 2 person group is .44 but a 4 person group is .68' (1969: 71-2).

Where the members of a group perform at a reasonably similar level then a larger group is more likely to represent the numbers accurately and to give a more stable estimate of the average than a small group. Obviously as increases in group size occur, more conflict is possible which may foster group performance but may equally hinder it. More resources are created (see 7 above), more opportunities for pairing and improving individual satisfactions occur, and more opportunities for members to hide or to gain respite from pressure are provided.

Large size has disadvantages of course, e.g. social obstacles tend to increase; subgroup formation can more easily get out of control and the aims such subgroups have are more frequently inconsistent with the over-all purpose of the large group. Although an increase in size increases the potential of groups there is a strong possibility that it will be wasted unless a change of organization or structure takes place to allow for the increase in members.

REFERENCES

Davis, J.H. (1969) *Group Performance.* Reading Mass.: Addison-Wesley.

Hare, A.P. (1962) *Handbook of Small Group Research.* N.Y.: Free Press

Henderson, J.A. and Leach, A. (1971) The 'Thursday Club' - an Experiment in Social Group Work. *Social Work Today* 1 (12): 21-4.

Hoffman, R. (1965) 'Group Problem-Solving'. In *Advances in Experimental Psychology.* (vol. II). N.Y.: Academic Press.

Krech, Crutchfield and Ballachey (1962) *Individual in Society.* N.Y.: McGraw Hill.

McGrath, J.E. and Altman, I. (1966) *Small Group Research: A Synthesis and Critique of the Field.* N.Y.: Holt, Rinehart and Winston.

Northen, H. (1970) *Social Work Groups.* Boulder, Col.: Col. U.P.

Schellenberg, J.A. (1959) 'Group Size as a Factor in the Success of Academic Discussion Groups'. *Journal of Educational Psychology* 13.

6

Observing, recording and evaluating

Very few social work texts pay any attention to the arts and skills necessary to record what goes on in a group successfully. Most of the available material therefore comes from the work of the group trainers who have recognized clearly that unless group proceedings are accurately recorded much of the value of the group will be lost.

The following material has been collected from many sources, the origins of some of which have been lost in the process of exchanging ideas, and it is hoped that it will give some idea of how the difficult task of recording a group at work may be done. In some instances the work of the group leader and the recorder are inextricably combined. It would be advisable, therefore, to refer to the section on leaders and co-leaders.

Perhaps the easiest and most effective way to learn about group behaviour is to observe a group while a member of it. Groups are a common experience for all people, but few have ever taken time to watch what was going on, or even to wonder why people behave as they do. It is hard sometimes to go against the cultural conditioning of appearing not to be curious, but increases in the ability to observe are very rewarding for the group practitioner.

Firstly it is necessary to distinguish between 'content' and 'process'. Content is usually described as the subject-matter under discussion - what the group is talking about. Process is the way in which the group goes about the discussion. In most group discussions the members are inevitably drawn by the words, the meanings, and tend not to notice the process which is involved i.e. who talks to whom, or how much. Focus on group process is looking at what the group is doing in the 'here and now', how it is working, its current procedures and organization. Focus on content is looking at the topics which may be largely abstract, oriented to the past, 'there and then', or the future, and not directly involving group members.

Obviously content serves often enough to give a clue to the process which is being involved. For example when group members are talking about staff who are of little help, the process involved may be dissatisfaction with the leader's role. Or again talking about the poor performance of other groups they are involved in may indicate the process of dissatisfaction with their own group's performance. Process can only really be understood by observing what is going on in the group and attempting to understand it in terms of what has occurred in the group previously.

Patterns of communication are a fairly easily observed group process. It is simple to record facts like who talks and for how long and how frequently. It is also easy enough to note in what direction people look when they talk, e.g. at other possible supporters, the whole group, or off into infinity. The communication process can be illuminated by noting who follows each speaker, where interruptions occur, and what styles are used e.g. questions, assertions, gesticulation and tone of voice. All of these factors may help to trace influence and power and the lack of them within the group.

Groups make decisions. As has been noted few people are able to assess clearly how a particular decision was reached unless forced into a painful memory by being questioned, e.g. police interrogation after an accident. But the decision-making process, in involving power, influence, knowledge, etc., is a very important group process and it is necessary that groups should know how important decisions are made. There is no more effective way of maintaining interest in a group's activities than for its decision-making processes to be clearly understood and usable by *all* members of the group. These processes must therefore be examined and the influence used at each stage clearly illuminated.

Democratic procedures, voting, testing opinions, polling are often used. But other procedures stemming from the exercise of personal influence or anxiety are much less easily seen. Groups are fond of saying, 'Well, we decided to do so and so', when it is quite obvious that they did not do this at all. If the incident is recent enough, memories may still exist when questioned about what really took place before the 'apparent' unanimous decision was made.

The three forms of group behaviour, task-oriented, maintenance-oriented and self-oriented have already been discussed in the section on leadership. Suffice it to say that these three behavioural orientations are found in all group members' behaviour and not just in leaders.

So far the discussion has been concerned with the way in which a group attempts to work, to achieve its purpose. But within any group there are emotional factors which may disrupt or adversely affect the work of the group. These factors need to be recognized and understood for they tend to detract from the energy which is available for the group's purpose. Some of these factors are identifiable, some attach to some stages of a group's life rather than others. For instance in the early days of a group's existence or during the admission of a newcomer the problem of identity may occur. Members are concerned to know where they fit in the group, and what kind of behaviour the group will accept and how they are coming across to the group. Later in the group's life they may be concerned with the problems related to power, control, and influence, in terms of knowing how much they have and whether holders of power are challengeable. Perhaps later still members will be concerned with intimacy, which is basically concerned with trust and personal involvement. Most of these factors have already been covered in the other sections but it is necessary to repeat them here because the manifest problems they can cause need to be recognized before appropriate action can be taken.

At most times a member will be concerned with the satisfaction of needs which he gets from the group. What he wants for the group and for himself may sometimes be in conflict, and keen observation is necessary in detecting the overt signs of this.

The behavioural patterns which emerge include resisting authority, attempting to satisfy individual needs at whatever cost to others, withdrawing from uncomfortable positions, and forming subgroups for support. Many other patterns occur and it is only with practice that the group worker can see them and become increasingly effective in his performance.

How to Diagnose Group Problems

(Extract from an article of this name by L.P. Bradford, D. Stock and M. Morwitz (1970). In Robert T. Golembiewski and Arthur Blumberg *Sensitivity Training and the Laboratory Approach.* Itasca, Ill.: F.E. Peacock).

Three most common group problems are:
1) *Conflict or fight*
2) *Apathy and non-participation*
3) *Inadequate decision-making*

Fight. Some ways in which fight can be expressed are:
a) members are impatient with one another
b) ideas are attacked before they are completely expressed
c) members take sides and refuse to compromise
d) members disagree on plans or suggestions
e) comments and suggestions are made with a great deal of vehemence
f) members attack one another on a personal level in subtle ways
g) members insist that the group doesn't have the know-how or experience to get anywhere
h) members feel that the group can't get ahead because it is too large or too small
i) members disagree with the leader's suggestions
j) members accuse one another of not understanding the real point
k) members hear distorted fragments of other members' contributions

The following are several possible reasons for such behaviour:
1) The group has been given an impossible job and members are frustrated because they feel unable to meet the demands made of them.

2) The main concern of members is to find status in the group. Although the group is ostensibly working on some task, the task is being used by the members as a means of jockeying for power.
3) Members are loyal to outside groups of conflicting interests.
4) Members feel involved and are working hard on a problem. Members may frequently express impatience, irritation, or disagreement because they have a real stake in the issue being discussed.

The obvious question arises: how can a member or leader tell which diagnosis is appropriate to a specific situation?

Let's re-examine our four descriptions of symptoms, this time in terms of possible diagnoses:

If:

every suggestion made seems impossible for practical reasons; some members feel the committee is too small; everyone seems to feel pushed for time;
members are impatient with one another;
members insist the group doesn't have the know-how or experience to get anywhere;
each member has a different idea of what the committee is supposed to do; whenever a suggestion is made, at least one member feels it won't satisfy the large organisation;

Then:

the group may have been given an impossible job and members are frustrated because they feel unable to meet the demands made of them, or the task is not clear or is disturbing.

If:

ideas are attacked before they are completely expressed; members take sides and refuse to compromise;
there is no movement towards a solution of the problem;
the group keeps getting stuck on inconsequential points;
members attack one another on a personal level in subtle ways;
there are subtle attacks on the leadership;
there is much clique formation;

Then:

the main concern of members may be in finding status in the group. The main interest is not in the problem. The problem is merely being used as a vehicle for expressing interpersonal concerns.

If:

the goal is stated in very general, non-operational terms;
members take sides and refuse to compromise;
each member is pushing his own plan;
suggestions don't build on previous suggestions, each member
seeming to start again from the beginning;
members disagree on plans or suggestions;
members don't listen to one another, each waiting for a chance
to say something;

Then:

each member is probably operating from a unique, unshared
point of view, perhaps because the members are loyal to
different outside groups with conflicting interests.

If:

there is a goal which members understand and agree on; most
comments are relevant to the problem;
members frequently disagree with one another over suggestions;
comments and suggestions are made with a great deal of
vehemence;
there are occasional expressions of warmth;
members are frequently impatient with one another;
there is general movement towards some solution of the problem;

Then:

probably, members feel involved and are working hard on a
problem;
the fight being expressed is constructive rather than destructive
in character and reflects real interest on the part of members.

2. *Apathy*

An apathetic membership is a frequent ailment of groups. Groups
may suffer in different degrees from this disease. In some cases
members may show complete indifference to the group task, and
give evidence of marked boredom. In others, apathy may take
the form of a lack of genuine enthusiasm for the job, a failure
to mobilise much energy, lack of persistence, satisfaction with
poor work.

Some ways in which apathy may be expressed:

a) frequent yawns, people dozing off
b) members lose the point of the discussion
c) low level of participation
d) conversation drags

e) members come late; are frequently absent
f) slouching and restlessness
g) overquick decisions
h) failure to follow through on decisions
i) ready suggestions for adjournment
j) failure to consider necessary arrangements for the next meeting
k) reluctance to assume any further responsibility.

Here are some of the common reasons for apathy:

1) The problem upon which the group is working does not seem important to the members, or it may seem less important than some other problem on which they would prefer to be working.

2) The problem may seem important to members, but there are reasons which lead them to avoid attempting to solve the problem. If members both desire to achieve a goal and fear attempting to achieve it, they are placed in a situation of conflict which may lead to tension, fatigue, apathy, e.g. where subordinates feel they will be punished for mistakes, they will avoid taking action, hoping to shift responsibility to someone higher up the line or organizational authority.

3) The group may have inadequate procedures for solving the problem. There may be lack of knowledge about the steps which are necessary to reach the goal. There may be poor communication among members within the group based on a failure to develop mutual understanding. There may be a poor co-ordination of effort so that contributions to the discussion are made in a disorganised, haphazard way.

4) Members may feel powerless about influencing final decisions.

5) A prolonged and deep fight among a few members has dominated the group. Frequently two or three dominant and talkative members of a group will compete with one another or with the leader so much that every activity in the group is overshadowed.

How to diagnose apathy:

If:

questions may be raised about what's really our job, what do they want us to do;

members fail to follow through on decisions;

there is no expectation that members will contribute responsibly, and confused, irrelevant statements are allowed to go by without question;

members wonder about the reason for working on this
problem, suggestions are made that we work on something
else;

the attitude is expressed that we should just decide on
anything, the decision doesn't really matter;

members seem to be waiting for a respectable amount of time
to pass before referring the decision to the leader, or to a
committee;

members are inattentive, seem to get lost and not to have
heard parts of the preceding discussion;

suggestions frequently 'plop', are not taken up and built on
by others;

no-one will volunteer for additional work;

Then:

the group goal may seem unimportant to the members.

If:

there are long delays in getting started, much irrelevant
preliminary conversation;

the group shows embarrassment or reluctance in discussing
the problem at hand;

members emphasise the consequence of making wrong
decisions, imagine dire consequences which have little
reference to ascertainable facts, members make suggestions
apologetically, are over-tentative, and hedge their
contributions with many if's and but's, solutions proposed
are frequently attacked as unrealistic, suggestions are made
that someone else ought to make the decision - the leader, an
outside expert, or some qualified person outside the group,
members insist that we haven't enough information or ability
to make a decision, and appear to demand an unrealistically
high level of competence;

the group has a standard of cautiousness in action, humorous
alternative proposals are suggested, with the group completely
unable to select among them;

Then:

members probably fear working toward the group goal.

If:

no-one is able to suggest the first step in getting started toward
the goal;

members seem to be unable to stay on a given point, and each person seems to start on a new track;

members appear to talk past, to misunderstand one another, and the same points are made over and over;

the group appears to be unable to develop adequate summaries, or restatements of points of agreement;

there is little evaluation of the possible consequences of decisions reached, and little attention is given to fact-finding or use of special resources;

members continually shift into related, but off-target tasks, complaints are made that the group's job is an impossible one, subgroups continually form around the table, with private discussions held off to the side, there is no follow-through on decisions or disagreement in the group on what the decisions really were;

complaints are made that you can't decide things in a group anyway, and the leader or somebody else should do the job;

Then:

the group may have inadequate problem-solving procedures.

If:

the view is expressed that someone else with more power in the organisation should be present in the meeting, that it is difficult to communicate with him at a distance, unrealistic decisions are made, and there is an absence of sense of responsibility for evaluation of the consequences of decisions, the position is taken that the decision doesn't really matter because the leader or someone else outside the group isn't really going to listen to what we say;

there is a tendency to ignore reaching consensus among members, the important thing being to get the leader to understand and listen, the discussion is oriented toward power relations, either within the group, jockeying to win over the leader, or outside the group, with interest directed toward questions about who really counts in the organisation; doubts are voiced about whether we're just wasting our efforts in working on this program;

members leave the meeting feeling they had good ideas which they didn't seem to be able to get across;

Then:

members feel powerless about influencing final decisions.

If:

two or three members dominate all discussion, but never agree;

conflict between strong members comes out no matter what is discussed;

dominant members occasionally appeal to others for support, but otherwise control conversation;

decisions are made by only two or three members,

Then:

a conflict among a few members is creating apathy in the others.

3. *Inadequate Decision-making*

Getting satisfactory decisions made is often a major struggle in the group. These problems are discussed in detail in the article *Decisions . . . Decisions . . . Decisions!* (not reprinted here). Here is a list of common symptoms of inefficient decision-making.

If:

the group swings between making too rapid decisions and having difficulty in deciding anything;

the group almost makes the decision but at the last minute retreats;

group members call for definition and redefinition of minute points;

the discussion wanders into abstraction;

Then:

there has been premature calling for a decision, or the decision is too difficult, or the group is low in cohesiveness and lacks faith in itself.

If:

the group has lack of clarity as to what the decision is, there is disagreement as to where consensus is;

a decision is apparently made but challenged at the end;

group members refuse responsibility;

there is continued effort to leave decision-making to leader, sub-group or outside source;

Then:

the decision area may be threatening to the group, either because of unclear consequences, fear of reaction of other groups, or fear of failure for the individuals.

Improving Group Efficiency - Diagnosis and Feedback
Human beings, and therefore groups, not only need continuous
self-correction in direction, but also (and here they differ from
machines) need to learn or grow or improve. Collecting adequate
data and using this information to make decisions about doing
things differently is one of the major ways of learning.

There are three basic parts to the process of changing group
behaviour:
1) collecting information
2) reporting the information to the group
3) making diagnoses and decisions for change.

Collecting information
While analysis and evaluation of information and decision about
what to do should be carried out by the total group, the collecting
of information may be delegated. A number of patterns of
delegation are possible:
1) The leader, serving also as observer, can report to the group
certain pertinent observations he has made about problems and
difficulties of group operation.
2) The group may appoint one of its members, perhaps on a
rotating basis, to serve as group observer, with the task of noting
the manner in which the group works.
3) A third method calls for all group members to be as sensitive
as they can, while participating actively, to the particular
problems the group faces.

What Information to Collect?
General questions such as these may help to get started:
1) What is our goal? Are we 'on' or 'off the beam'?
2) Where are we in our discussion? At the point of analysing the
problem? Suggesting solutions? Testing ideas?
3) How fast are we moving? Are we bogged down?
4) Are we using the best methods of work?
5) Are all of us working or just a few?
6) Are we making any improvement in our ability to work
together?

Methods of Observation
1) Who talks to whom?

Figure 4

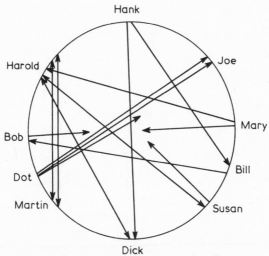

The number of lines made by the observer on this form indicates the number of statements made in a fifteen minute period - 20. Four of these were made to the group as a whole, and so the arrows go only to the middle of the circle. Those with arrows at each end of a line show that the statement made by one person to another was reponded to by the recipient.

We see that one person, Harold, had more statements directed toward him than did anyone else and that he responded or participated more than anyone else.

2) Who makes what kinds of contributions?

Table 5

Member No.	1	2	3	4	5	6	7	8	9	10
1 Encourages										
2 Agrees, accepts										
3 Arbitrates										
4 Proposes action										
5 Asks suggestions										
6 Gives opinion										
7 Asks opinion										
8 Gives information										
9 Seeks information										
10 Poses problem										
11 Defines position										
12 Asks position										
13 Routine direction										
14 Depreciates self										
15 Autocratic manner										
16 Disagrees										
17 Self-assertion										
18 Active aggression										
19 Passive aggression										

* Based upon observation categories discussed in R.F. Bales (1950). *Interaction Process Analysis*. Reading, Mass.: Addison-Wesley.

This record makes possible the quick rating not only of who talked, but the type of contribution. Individuals in the group are given numbers which are listed at the top of the columns. At the end of a time period it is possible to note the frequency and type of participation by each member.

1. *What was the general atmosphere in the group?*
   Formal................................ Informal ....
   Competitive........................ Co-operative ....
   Hostile............................... Supportive..................................
   Inhibited .... Permissive.................................
   Comments..

2. *Quantity and quality of work accomplished*
   Accomplishment: High .... Low ....
   Quality of
   Production: High .... Low ....
   Goals: Clear........................ Vague ....
   Methods: Clear........................ Vague ....
   Comments..

3. *Leadership behaviour*
   Attentive to group needs ....
   Supported others..
   Concerned only with topic.................. Took sides....................
   Dominated group .... Helped group.....................
   Comments..

4. *Participation*
   Most people talked.............. Only few talked..........................
   Members involved................ Members apathetic ....
   Group united........................ Group divided.............................
   Comments..
   This form can be used as a checklist by an observer to sum up
   his observations, or it can be filled out by all group members to
   start an evaluation discussion.

An example of the evaluation of a group using a very simple
questionnaire is given below. It is taken from *Group for Mothers*
by Brown and Smith (1972).

'*Evaluation*
At the last session we distributed evaluation forms. Those who
were not present or had previously dropped out were sent forms
by post. A total of fifteen mothers were given forms. Of the
seven most regular members, six returned them, and two of the

other mothers who had dropped out returned theirs. Members were asked the following questions:

1) Before you came to the group what did you expect it to be like?

2) Was the group different from what you expected?

3) Have you any suggestions for the leaders?

4) Do you have any comments about meeting time, place, length of sessions, child-minding, or any other practical considerations?

5) If another group were to start in the future would you be interested in participating?

In summarising the evaluations we have used the following extracts.

One mother wrote that she expected the group to be "rather formal with speakers and possibly visitors from the welfare department to talk to us". Instead she found it "far more informal and friendly. One feels one can bring into the open one's personal feelings and opinions". Another who had had a very difficult time with the behaviour of her five year old subnormal son said "I do not know quite why, but I thought the meetings might be very dull and felt attending them every week would be too often. I did not expect the lively and human discussions we did have". In fact she found the meetings

"... much more interesting than I had expected. I learnt a very great deal by attending the group meetings and derived much comfort and encouragement from the group. After the meetings, however, I must confess, I often felt sad and upset at the knowledge of some of the mothers' problems. I do feel strongly that although the group meetings are of very real value to mothers concerned, they should have the wider aim of establishing an effective link between parents, teachers and the children at school. Perhaps a Parent-Teacher Association is not appropriate at this stage, but certainly meetings of any future group should be mainly concerned with the problems of forwarding the children's progress both at school and at home ..."

A third highly articulate mother, whose son regularly spends all the holidays at the subnormality hospital and who appeared to have made the "perfect" adjustment to a handicapped child, expected "a group of fairly inarticulate mothers airing their complaints about doctors and help offered from various sources", but found the mothers had a "positive approach to their problem and not a negative one. They are able to discuss family emotions and compare methods of dealing with problems". She felt the leaders' function was to "control the group, as involved outsiders, and to help keep the thread of an interesting line of discussion".

Another of the regular members, herself and her husband both artists and whose only child is autistic, wrote that she "expected the group to be different - rather formal". She found it "very informal and a pleasant atmosphere". She concluded "I must stress that it gave me a tremendous satisfaction of being able to express my feelings about the problems that I have or rather had, as it is easier now because I have shared it with others".

One mother who is a nurse had very negative feelings towards the services and only attended two groups: she wrote that she wished the group had dealt with such things as times and places of coach pick-ups for school so that these could be more convenient for mothers.

In the above account we have discussed the creation of the group and presented statistics about selection and membership as well as methods and results of evaluation.' (1972: 16).

Evaluating Information and Deciding about Change

Usually this has a number of steps:
1) The members assess the observations, relate them to their experience, test to see whether they agree with the report.
2) The group examines the reasons. What caused a thing to happen? Could we have recognized it earlier?
3) The group moves to a decision on what to do. What can be done in future similar circumstances? What can individual members do earlier to help? What methods or procedures should be changed? What new directions sought?

It is very easy for the time of the discussion to be consumed by the first two steps in this procedure. The leader, as well as the members, needs to be sensitive to this danger and encourage the group to move into the third step of decision. A questionnaire like the 'Yardstick' can be used to facilitate this process.

A Yardstick for Measuring the Growth of a Group

As a group begins its life, and at several points during its growth, the leader and members might individually fill out the following scales and then spend some time sharing the data that is collected. Through these scales, it is possible to get a general picture of the perceptions which various members have about the group and how it is growing. It is also possible to pick up areas in which there may be some difficulties which are blocking progress.

Table 6

1. *How clear are the group goals?*

1.	2.	3.	4.	5.
No apparent goals	Goal confusion, uncertainty, or conflict	Average goal clarity	Goals mostly clear	Goals very clear

2. *How much trust and openness in the group?*

1.	2.	3.	4.	5.
Distrust, a closed group	Little trust, defensiveness	Average trust and openness	Considerable trust and openness	Remarkable trust and openness

3. *How sensitive and perceptive are group members?*

1.	2.	3.	4.	5.
No awareness or listening in the group	Most members self-absorbed	Average sensitivity and listening	Better than usual listening	Outstanding sensitivity to others.

4. *How much attention was paid to process? (the way group was working)*

1.	2.	3.	4.	5.
No attention to process	Little attention to process	Some concern with group process	A fair balance between content and process	Very concerned with process

5. *How were group leadership needs met?*

1.	2.	3.	4.	5.
Not met, drifting	Leadership concentrated in one person	Some leadership sharing	Leadership functions distributed	Leadership needs met creatively and flexibly

6. *How were group decisions made?*

1.	2.	3.	4.	5.
No decisions could be reached	Made by a few	Majority vote	Attempts at integrating minority vote	Full participation and tested consensus

7. *How well were group resources used?*

1.	2.	3.	4.	5.
One or two contributed but deviants silent	Several tried to contribute but were discouraged	About average use of group resources	Group resources well used and encouraged	Group resources fully and effectively used

8. *How much loyalty and sense of belonging to the group?*

1.	2.	3.	4.	5.
Members had no group loyalty or sense of belonging	Members not close but some friendly relations	About average sense of belonging	Some warm sense of belonging	Strong sense of belonging among members

(G. L. Lippitt and E.W. Seashore)

'Evaluation of the progress of members is made more precise and easier for the worker if some plan is developed for tracing changes in attitudes, relationships, and behaviour periodically during the course of the group experience. Perhaps minimally summary reports should be made at the end of the first meeting, toward the end of the exploration phase, and when termination is being considered. The first report would include pertinent data about the individual; his characteristics, problems, capacities and motivations; goals as seen by the member, relevant others who may have referred him, and the worker; and an initial description and evaluation of the member's beginning in the group. As changes occur, these can be noted from week to week or periodically. These changes are usually those in attitudes toward self and others, changes in the quality and range of social relationships, and changes in problematic behaviour. Necessary data are then available for the practitioner to assist him to understand and evaluate the nature and extent of progress and regression. The movement of each individual is evaluated in relation to the trend of changes within the group, and the impact of environmental influences on it . . . whenever termination is being considered, a thorough review and evaluation of what has or has not been accomplished, and the determinants thereof, is imperative. So, too, is a set of realistic goals for the periods of time that remain before the final termination.'

(Northen, 1969: 224-5).

Recording

The recorder acts as a 'group memory', by recording important parts of the discussion, and by summarizing its content.

He reminds the group what is under consideration when the discussion wanders and can assist communication between different groups.

He is a member of the group, and assists in the problem-solving task by working as a member of the team with the leader and co-leader. He also ensures that the group does not lose valuable material and he tends to free the leader from the very onerous task of record-keeping but this usually means reducing the effective contribution of the recorder as a member of the group. These points are elaborated upon below.

The recorder is in a sense an aid to the group memory. Everyone else in the group is freer to participate, if he knows that a specialized 'memory' is at work, seeing that the ideas and decisions that are being produced are stored up for later use. Every group needs a summary from time to time of what it has done, of where it stands in relation to the goals it has or the problem it has defined. Groups may wish to ask the recorder to make this kind of summary.

A group with continuing records of its various meetings may use these in the evaluation of its progress from meeting to meeting and in analysing and improving its productivity.

The records of ideas and decisions and their relation to each other are a significant and vital part of the resources of a group. The record of group thinking should be summarized in closely related paragraphs or outline units. Ideas developed over an extended period of discussion may be phrased in a simple pointed sentence or paragraph. Conflicting ideas should be reported as well as those showing consensus as these may be valuable in future deliberations on the group's problems. Verbatim records are rarely necessary but a clear exposition of the basic content of the group discussion is essential.

It is recommended that:

a) recording should be made selectively.

b) pages of the report might be kept for different areas of content e.g. Problems, Agreements, Decisions, Ideas, etc. Summaries, when required, are easier to make from organized source material.

c) issues, points of assent and dissent, and what conclusion is arrived at should be clearly noted.

d) the accuracy of the record should be checked out with the group.

e) some such form of headings as the following should be used:

Date	Group Session	
Subject	Content	Decisions

f) evaluation of the record by the group should be asked for along the lines of how much was left out, what was put in that was not needed and perhaps how the form of the record should be improved.

g) organization of the record should take place as it is recorded in order to be available to the group when needed.

h) underlining and other symbols should be used to distinguish various parts of the content.

i) the recording should be available to the group whenever requested to check its progress.

j) the recorder should stick to the content of the group's activities. 'Process' is the responsibility of the co-leader.

k) the group should be asked to correct, amend, and check the record whenever doubt exists.

l) the recorder should attempt to summarize for the group in the same terms as have already been used. Where semantic change occurs the recorder should check that the group's original meaning has not been changed.

m) the recorder should be involved in the planning phases with leader and co-leader, especially over what records may be required.

REFERENCES

Bales, R. F. (1950) *Interaction Process Analysis.* Reading, Mass.: Addison Wesley.

Brown, L.K. and Smith, J. (1972) Group for Mothers. *Social Work Today* 3 (10): 16.

Bradford, L.P. Stock, D. and Morwitz, M. (1970). How to diagnose group problems. In Robert T. Golembiewski and Arthur Blumberg *Sensitivity Training and the Laboratory Approach: Readings about Concepts and Applications.* Itasca, Ill.: F.E. Peacock.

Lippitt, G.L. and Seashore, E.W. *The Leader looks at Group Effectiveness.* (Pamphlet).

Northen, H. (1969) *Social Work with Groups.* Boulder, Col.: Col. Univ. Press.

7

Conflict and confrontation

Conflict is an essential ingredient of human existence. Frequently this basic fact is overlooked because excessive conflict is seen to create hardship, promote aggressors, and to produce great hurt.

'Realistic conflict is tied to a rational goal and the conflict concerns the means of achieving the goal. In unrealistic conflict the conflict becomes the end in itself.'

(Northen, 1969: 42).

Northen also comments on the fact that conflict within a group can lead to increased understanding and an increase in trust, largely because differences are brought out into the open and cease to be a source of hidden irritation. This is closely related to the concept of 'unfinished business'.

Golembiewski and Blumberg describe this as follows:

A. becomes aware of a feeling or thought about himself or others and does not disclose this information. This enlarges the "Hidden Area", and accumulates what is called 'unfinished business". That business acts as an unresolved tension system that interferes with the individual's ability to operate effectively and congruently in relation to others. By the same token, if A's behaviour hinders B - blocks him from behaving congruently with his feelings for example - B develops unfinished business with A and increases the "Blind Area" until he openly deals with A's unawareness.

Perhaps the simplest way of representing unfinished business and the blind and hidden areas referred to is the Jo-Hari Window. Named after its two originators, Joseph Luft and Harry Ingram, 'The window divides a person's life awareness into four areas, utilizing the dimensions "Known to self" and "Known to others" to characterize knowledge about what a person is and how he appears to others'.

(Golembiewski and Blumberg, 1970: 60-1).

Figure 5 *Jo-Hari Window*

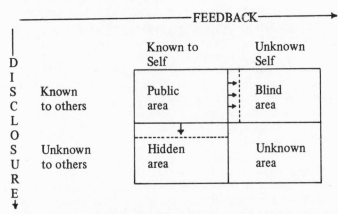

Blind areas comprise behaviour which others can see but of which the individual is unaware.

Hidden areas comprise behaviour which the individual keeps to himself.

A decrease of the blind area occurs by the individual receiving 'feedback' from others - a decrease of the hidden area occurs when the individual discloses himself to others, becomes more known.

Unexpected insights may reduce the unknown area.

The enlargement of the public area increases awareness and opens behaviour to an element of conscious choice in areas previously restricted or out of such control.

Napier and Gershenfeld (1973) suggest that an individual

attempts to bring his life into a state of equilibrium. In this balanced state he then becomes able to predict what will occur and is thus able to reduce conflict. Obviously when a group is being used as a 'change agent', as most groups are, conflict arises as members resist the threat they see to stable and predictable relationships. That such change could be beneficial takes time to accept.

It is possible to show that in group situations conflict may arise from several major areas. For instance when personal needs and purposes are different to the accepted needs and purpose of the group a strong sense of frustration may well develop into conflict in order to achieve a higher level of personal satisfaction. Most of the problems concerned with acceptance, with power and its use, and with liking, all contain the seeds of possible conflict. Decision-making contains endless possibilities of conflict, most of it probably useful in motivating discussion and in powering the action based on whatever decision is reached, but inevitably there will be a residue of conflict not absorbed in this way which will spill over into personal relationships. New behaviours by group members, frustrations caused by not enough time to air one's view or by there being too many people, all may be sources of conflict.

In the diagram below which is a model of decision-making, the process clearly indicates conflicting ideas being fed in. Different opinions, ideas, information ensure that much more of the problem is offered for debate and then there is less possibility of a decision being taken on either inadequate information and ideas or by being pushed through ignoring contradictory data.

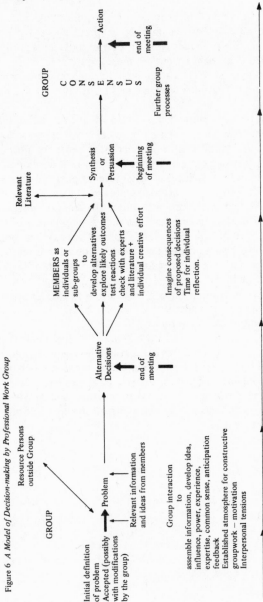

Figure 6 *A Model of Decision-making by Professional Work Group*

Miles says 'A group without conflict may be in serious difficulty, points of view are being masked and inhibited, and good solutions cannot be worked out.' He points out that it becomes very necessary to distinguish between disabling disagreement and that conflict which 'enriches problem-solving and productivity.' (1959): 25.

Konopka (1963) agrees with this verdict but adds that a group constantly in a state of conflict with no way out is a very 'sick' group indeed.

Both Konopka and Northen give six ways of solving conflict in the group situation. They are given below in a combined form:
1) elimination (forced withdrawal)
2) subjugation
3) compromise
4) integration
5) minority consent to majority rule (alliance)
6) majority rule.

Very obviously conflict solution is a specific function of a group. 'The essence of conflict is difference' says Northen and goes on to point out that no resolution is possible until a given group has a 'solid basic consensus' upon which to work. Change and crisis are frequently the bases of conflict as has already been stated. Herrick (1966) produced a model (see below) illustrating exactly this kind of conflict and its resolution:

Figure 7

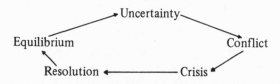

From the state of equilibrium uncertainty is generated which leads to conflict. Resolution takes place through effective problem solving.

It is now appropriate to look at confrontation as a method of dealing with conflict and providing a resolution and establishing group equilibrium at a different level.

Confrontation says Golembiewski and Blumberg:

> attempts to encourage group participants to join in a mutual
> escalation of truthfulness, so as to reverse degenerative
> feedback sequences. It has a compelling internal logic which
> encourages owning and openness concerning organisational
> issues, with the goals of increasing mutual trust and decreasing
> the perceived risk of owning and being open.

Concealment is bred into people. The frankness and honesty
of a small child, who has not yet been trained to hide what he
knows or sees for fear of sanctions, frequently reveals how
basically dishonest human relations have become. Why should
honesty hurt more than deceit? Politeness, cultural norms,
patterns of superior/inferior relationships all overlie and obscure
an already poor level of honest communication. The energy
which is used to maintain and fight for deceits may well be
better used in establishing authentic relationships. Conflict often
arises from unrevealed sources of irritation, which if they had
been cleared would not have been able to fuel such a conflict.

Rose writing about punishment says 'one common practice,
however, in the face of persistent deviant behaviour, is
confrontation of the deviant by peer reaction.' (1973). Rose
sees confrontation used in this way as a kind of punishment and
certainly it must be admitted that confrontation is seldom a
pleasurable experience. It is usually met with strong resistance
in order to maintain equilibrium, but in the face of the number of
people involved it is very hard to resist and a group member
may find himself confronted by feedback from his colleagues
of the way in which they perceive his behaviour.

Napier and Gershenfeld put this very succinctly:

> 'The confrontation approach to personal growth is based on
> the assumption that a person needs to be shaken out of
> previous patterns, awakened from his lethargy, and made to
> face his own self-created realities. Because we are encased in
> defences of our own creation, it is believed that they cannot
> be smoothed away and that it requires more than gentleness
> and understanding to grasp the true self from which we have
> been hiding. Only then will a person have a chance to
> visualise alternative behavioural patterns that may

strengthen and enrich his life.' (1973: 272-3).

In *Small Group Psychotherapy* (1971), the authors discuss the use of confrontation in a crisis situation in terms of 'milieu therapy'. A crisis, they maintain, amongst people working together can be brought to a beneficial resolution by the use of face-to-face confrontation. In the light of cool, clear reason the reports of a situation given by the various participants in it are frequently quite disparate, as witness the reports given by observers of traffic accidents. How much more then can it be expected that in a crisis situation emotionally loaded, distorted communication takes place.

A good example of how conflict can arise within a group, in this case a residential group, and how confrontation may be used to deal with it is given in the extract below from Breslin and Sturton:

'The first really difficult issue brought to the group arose from a change within the hostel. Five of the residents were to move out to a new unstaffed house nearby - with their agreement of course. The following record of part of the meeting where this was discussed was written by the groupworker.

"When I arrived at the hostel Ann approached me to say that she and four of the others would be moving out at the weekend into the new unstaffed hostel. I encouraged her to raise this in the meeting . . . Before the session began there was an incident in the office where Doris rushed in demanding that a member of staff wash her hair for her. She was told quite firmly that she was capable of doing this for herself. She became very upset and went off crying. I gathered that she was another of the candidates for the unstaffed hostel, and was reacting to the prospect of moving out (though she had opted for the move) by making excessive demands on the staff . . .

I went into the meeting room ahead of the staff, to find everyone assembled and listening in silence to Doris, who was crying noisily and saying something betweeen sobs. She stopped talking when she saw me but went on crying. There was a pause, and I encouraged her to continue. She explained she was not going to the house after all - she'd changed her mind. It took a lot of work to sort out why. At intervals she would revert to sobs again, and I appealed to the others to help her say what was troubling her, if they knew. Gradually the problem emerged: Doris' friend Muriel, who was not moving out, was 'being mean' to Doris. The rest of the group confirmed this. Doris could not stand being tormented - she would rather stay at the hostel.

Unfortunately Muriel was out for the evening, so could not defend herself. The feeling against her mounted higher, and it seemed she was being scapegoated for the others' anxieties and jealousies. Eventually Iris shouted out 'You are all being unfair to Muriel' and burst into tears herself. A few others began to cry too. I said to Iris It seems you are saying the change in the hostel is hard on Muriel as well as Doris - maybe Muriel is upset too'. Iris agreed. We went on to discuss, bit by bit, all the feelings involved. How did those who were moving out feel? Pride, fear, excitement in general were identified. Mrs. Breslin, who was in the meeting by now, helped the five concerned talk about their plans for the house - the tasks they would have, how they would do the cooking, and so on. She was firm in getting each individual resident to speak for herself, since the more managing ones of the five tended to take over and allot the less pleasant jobs to the weaker residents, in anticipation. A calmer atmosphere permeated the meeting. We went on to encourage the residents who were staying behind to say how they felt. Jealousy, indifference, relief, at not being faced with this challenging change - all these feelings seemed to be present. Discussion was slow, and there was a lot of silence.

We tried to suggest there was a connection between some of them being 'mean' to each other, and all these feelings they had. It was hard to judge how much of this was understood, but Doris, who had been the focus for distress in the Group, said she would go to the hostel after all. . ."

This meeting demonstrated to the residents that deep and disturbing feelings could be shared and to some extent relieved within the group. The five set up house successfully, and there were no major difficulties around their departure. We learnt something about helping the group handle sensitive areas of emotion through this session and subsequent ones. The residents often seemed to be caught up in conflicting feelings, only one of which they could put a name to. It was therefore important to help them recognise and define all their emotions, and work out the causes of distress where possible. A patient process of unravelling the meanings behind tears or anger or silence must take place. It is vital too to involve the rest of the group in this, because often they have the clues to the disturbance or can recognise what is happening from their own experience. Encouraging the group to think about an individual's problem and identify feelings and worries help to develop the greater sensitivity towards others that the staff were hoping for. Of course, these techniques are used in groupwork with other clients, but it seems especially important in this setting. To let the residents flit uneasily and super-ficially over a range of ill-defined feelings leads to frustration, sometimes masked by apparent boredom or withdrawal.

Since the session described above, the meetings have covered many topics, painful and joyful. Residents have talked of their feelings at being abandoned or ignored by their families, and have shared their sense of loss over having to leave home when a parent or relative died. Relationships with boyfriends, and the implications of marriage, have also been discussed, though with some inhibition. Conflicts between residents have come into the open. The main irritant seems to be the unavoidable sharing of rooms — disagreements become almost intolerable in this situation. Sometimes it is possible to arrange a swop to help the tension; sometimes alterations in sleeping arrangements are impossible, or have been tried many times before. In the end the group may be left with no alter-native but to reflect on how hard it is to live en masse, after noting the conflict and ensuring that each party has had her say. This in itself seems to ease the tension.

The meetings have also been used to plan further activities, or discuss possible outings. We are careful to follow through and ask for reports on how people found the outings — were they enjoyable, could different plans have been made?

Occasionally a resident is unable to take part in something strenuous, like swimming, because of a disability or a tendency to have fits: the group shows great understanding in these instances. A few suggestions have been made about changes within the hostel, and where feasible these have been put into practice. The staff welcome such suggestions, and are careful to explain why some ideas are impractical or too expensive.' (Breslin and Sturton 1974: 722-6)

Confrontation consists of bringing together all the major participants in the crisis situation, omitting no-one so that the balance is maintained, and eliciting all the various points of view. Timing is important and the confrontation should take place as soon as possible after the crisis incident so that defensive tactics will not have had time to solidify and to take the steam out of the situation.

Skilled leadership is necessary to aim at clarification and to demonstrate how communication lines have been tangled. Frequently expected responses have not been forthcoming and misinterpretations of verbal and non-verbal cues have created confusion, anxiety, and anger. If members can be encouraged to recall their feelings and expectations, most often the confrontation demonstrates with remarkable clarity the assumptions, upon which response and action were based, to have been inaccurate to say the least.

Skilled leadership must also offer the security which is essential to the effective operation of confrontation. No member of a group can feel safe in volunteering his true feelings into the group pool if he is in any way anxious about the confidentiality and absolute security of the setting in which he volunteers them. If it becomes a norm of the group that such confrontations are confined to the group session and that all who take part are free from outside reprisals then the confrontation stands a great possibility of successfully freeing the members from the hang-ups engendered in the crisis situation.

Feedback may develop into 'confrontations'. Carl Rogers gives a very good example of this:

There are times when the term 'feedback' is far too mild to describe the interactions which take place, when it is better said that one individual *confronts* another, directly, "levelling" with him. Such confrontations can be positive, but frequently they are decidedly negative, as the following example will make abundantly clear. In one of the last sessions of a group, Alice had made some quite vulgar and contemptuous remarks to John, who was entering religious work. The next morning, Norma, who had been a very quiet person in the group, took the floor:

Norma (loud sigh): "Well, I don't have *any* respect for you, Alice. *None!* (pause) There's about a hundred things going through my mind, I want to say to you, and by God I hope I get through 'em all. First of all, if you wanted us to respect you, then why couldn't you respect John's feelings last night? Why have you been on him today? Hmm? Last night — couldn't you — couldn't you accept — *couldn't you* comprehend in any way at all that — that *he felt* his unworthiness in the service of God? Couldn't you accept this, or did you have to dig into it today to find something *else there?* And his respect for womanhood — he *loves* women — yes, he does, because he's a real person, but you — you're not a real woman — to me — and thank God you're not my mother!!! I want to come over and beat the hell out of you!!! I want to slap you across the mouth so hard and — oh, and you're so, you're so many years above me — and I respect age, and I respect people who are older than me, *but I don't respect you, Alice at all.* And I was *so hurt* and *confused* because you love making someone else feel *hurt* and *confused . . ."*

It may relieve the reader to know that these two women came to accept each other, not completely, but much more understandingly, before the end of the session. But this *was* a confrontation. (1972:200-201)

Confrontation can be seen to be an effective technique for coping with unfinished business and thus rooting out the possible bases of future unrewarding blocking and unproductive conflict. Essentially it must take place in a safe environment where members of the group feel secure enough and trusting enough to accept that the pressure being applied has ultimately a beneficial awareness-creating end.

Napier and Gershenfeld (1973: 272-3) list eight possible dangers in the use of this method as follows:

(1) its use becomes indiscriminate
(2) the approach can become ritualistic
(3) members may feel victimized or used and react against it
(4) not all people have the same needs or make the same responses
(5) members can find themselves stripped of defences with no alternatives available
(6) members may have no time to 'internalize' newly acquired insights and behaviours
(7) the support of the group may not be constantly available
(8) members may have greater fears than previously.

Like all group methods this one needs handling with sensitivity and understanding particularly of the strengths that members have upon which they can draw. Some of the dangers given above are self-evident. Even the most effective technique used too often can become an evasive, avoidance ritual which members perform because it has become the accepted norm. The results of such rituals may enhance cohesion but they seldom if ever achieve the enlightenment and personal growth they were designed to enhance. 'Differences between persons or groups in organisations can be handled in a variety of ways including avoidance, repression and indirect conflict. A more direct approach to conflict involves confrontation, hopefully leading toward problem solving'. (Walton, 1970: 829).

REFERENCES

Breslin, A. and Sturton, S. (1974) Groupwork in a Hostel for the Mentally Handicapped. *Social Work Today* 4(23): 722-26.

Golembiewski, R.T. and Blumberg, A. (eds.) (1970) *Sensitivity Training and the Laboratory Approach* Itasca. Ill.: F.E. Peacock.

Herrick, J.C. (1966) *The Perception of Crisis in Modified Therapeutic Community.* (Unpublished D.S.W. disseration). Sch. Soc. Work, University of S. California.

Konopka, G. (1963) *Social Group Work: A Helping Process.* Englewood Cliffs., N.J.: Prentice-Hall.

Napier, R.W. and Gershenfeld, M.K. (1973) *Groups: Theory and Experience.* Boston: Houghton Mifflin Co.

Northen, H. (1969) *Social Work with Groups*. Boulder, Col.: Col. U.P.

Miles, M.B. (1959) *Learning to Work in Groups*. Col. Uni. N.Y.: Teachers' Coll. Press.

Rogers, C.R. (1972) The Process of the Basic Encounter Group. In Diedrich, R.C. and Dye, H.A. (eds.) *Group Procedures: Purposes, Processes and Outcomes*. Boston: Houghton Mifflin Co.

Rose, S.D. (1973) *Treating Children in Groups*. London: Jossey-Bass.

Walton, H. (ed.) (1971) *Small Group Psychotherapy*. Harmondsworth: Penguin.

Walton, R.E. (1970) Interpersonal Confrontation and Basic Third Party Functions: A Case Study. In Golembiewski, R.T. and Blumberg, A. (eds.) *Senstivity Training and the Laboratory Approach*. Itasca, Ill.: F.E. Peacock.

8

Membership of a group

It may be trite to say that the members of a group bring to it their previous experience and share with one another the experience of being part of a group. The members *are* the group: the influence of the group upon them may be great or small, but one thing is certain, there are influences at work, whatever the experience and knowledge of the individual may be.

Experimenters have been concerned to show what can happen to the individual who joins a particular group. They have pointed out that his experience and his abilities, his personality, his background, his attitudes, in fact everything he brings to the group will interact with what other people bring to it and that out of this interaction will arise a unique on-going situation which will be this particular group. Thus, it would appear that what people are in a group situation may be very important in deciding whether the group is effective.

One fact which has consistently emerged from this kind of experimental datum is that it is not easy to predict the performance of a particular group from the knowledge of the abilities of the individual members. McGrath and Altman say 'The differential relationship of member abilities to individual versus group performance certainly highlights the old question of whether individuals *summate* to form a group or whether the characteristics of individual members combine in some nonadditive but otherwise unknown way.' (1966: 56). We just do not know enough about how member abilities and potential are 'transformed' into effective group performance.

An area concerning members which has had quite a lot of coverage concerns the attractiveness of a given group for an individual member. There are two sides to this coin, i.e. the member or potential member is attracted by the group, or he perceives that he can increase his satisfactions by becoming or continuing as a member. Obviously the two are directly related; a group becomes more attractive to the individual member as it enhances the satisfaction he gets from it. But it is as well to consider the negative aspect of this also, that decrease in satisfaction will also decrease the group's attractiveness. If this continues beyond a certain point then alternative situations will become more attractive and the member will tend to leave.

In created groups, brought together for some express purpose, the nature of member satisfaction may be very hard to define and probably very complex. Where no apparent compulsion to remain exists, it is often surprising that some people remain in the group. The fear of leaving, ridicule, no available alternative, all may be involved . Where compulsion to remain is involved, then satisfaction has to be sought in different ways and is available at different levels.

Member Satisfaction

In order to investigate member satisfaction, two writers reviewed a large number of research findings. They isolated three variables as being mainly associated with member satisfaction. These are:
(1)   status consensus
(2)   perception of progress toward group goals, and
(3)   perceived freedom to participate.

Primarily, these factors indicate that member satisfaction is high when all are agreed about their position and standing within the group, when progress and achievement are readily observed and when each member is keenly aware that he is in no way restricted from joining all the group's activities in the way he wishes and up to the level he desires. Of course, these conditions are Utopian, but the degree of their achievement must relate quite closely to the degree of satisfaction members feel in the group.

Heslin and Dunphy (1964), however, are not content to show that these variables exist and influence member satisfaction, but go on to postulate how the variables might be used to increase member satisfaction in the family group, the therapy group, and the formal organization group. Most importantly, the authors indicate that an examination of members' expectations and their apparent reality might be followed by an attempt to change either the expectations or the situation.

In the therapy situation the authors apply their thesis to groups conducted in the manner of Bion and point out that the therapist seems to be deliberately manipulating 'status consensus' and 'good achievement' to decrease member satisfaction in the early stages of the group's existence. Finally, they show the application of their thesis to formal organizations like business concerns.

This paper is remarkable in that it is one of a very small number of research papers which makes any effort to show the direct implication of applying what has been discovered during the research. It is very evident in family therapy, for instance, that status consensus occupies a very important place. The therapist attempts to induce the family members to recognize the discrepancies between their expectations of the positions they believe they hold and the way others experience them. A narrowing of the discrepancies results in an increase in satisfaction and tends to establish a more harmonious existence.

The discussion in Heslin and Dunphy's article is quoted in full in the light of the amount of interesting material it contains:

'We can therefore conclude that variations in the three variables we have isolated operate to influence member satisfaction in all fully fledged group situations. However, we feel that a scheme such as this should not only draw together the results of existing experimental and observational studies, but should also contribute to our understanding by generating means of improving member satisfaction in more permanent groups. Accordingly, three groups of major significance in social life today – the nuclear family, the therapy group, and the formal organization group — will be examined to indicate the usefulness of this scheme.

Parsons & Bales (1955) have stressed that the basic functions of the nuclear family are two: "First, the primary socialization of children . . . : second, the stabilization of the adult personalities of the population of the society". The family may be characterized therefore as a small group whose major goals are providing for many of the important generalized social-emotional needs of the members and the socialization of the children. Accordingly, in relation to participation we may postulate that the satisfaction of family members will be reduced when: (i) the family fails to meet the level of member expectations, socially or emotionally (e.g. respect, humor, intimacy): (ii) family members perceive that they have little freedom to participate in deciding on or implementing important family concerns. In relation to goal attainment we may postulate that member satisfaction will tend to be reduced when: (iii) the family fails to maintain the expected rate of progress in socializing a child or children (e.g. low school grades, delinquency) and/or does not maintain its expected position among the other families which it uses as a larger reference group. Similarly, in relation to status consensus we may postulate that the satisfaction of family members will be reduced when: (iv) there is lack of consensus about the relative status of family members and particularly about the relative status of the parents (high-status persons).

With regard to points (i) and (iii) above, we feel that supportive evidence is unnecessary since a few moments' reflection will bring to mind many experiences which confirm them. In regard to (ii) and (iv), it is interesting that these points are paralleled by two schools of child-rearing theory: one which advocates permissive child-rearing practices emphasizing the children's participation in decisions concerning the family group as a whole (the child should be both seen and heard); and the other recommending the importance of a clear authority differential with the father as unquestionable head of the family. It appears to us that from the point of view of the satisfaction of family members both approaches have values — one stressing member participation and the other status consensus. It seems likely that the tendency for popular support to swing, pendulum fashion, from one position to the other indicates the necessity of recognizing both variables. In addition, the widespread feeling that one parent is never an adequate substitute for two indicates that the "great parent" is even more rare than the "great man" leader, and that the more usual way of achieving status consensus in the family, as elsewhere, is by establishing two differentiated and mutually supportive roles. The same principles which create a high level of satisfaction in other types of group appear also to operate in the family.

In efforts to change families in order to increase member satisfaction, such as occur in marriage guidance or counselling, we suggest the usefulness of examining members' expectations on the three variables and of taking steps either to change the expectations or to change the external or internal structure of the family until the situation approximates the expectations.

The therapy or training group represents an interesting example of our thesis, since in this case particular variables are manipulated by the trainer (or therapist) to produce certain desired effects. Here the members are faced from the first session with a leader who will not assume the usual authority role. Those who normally establish a dependent or counter-dependent relationship with a group leader find it impossible to create such a relationship. Doubts occur as to the leader's capability as a trainer and the resulting frustration reactions are used by the trainer to understand member motivations and to force the members to recognize these motivations. Member satisfaction in the early stages of such groups is notoriously low (e.g. see Bion, 1961) and we suggest that the reasons for this are as follows:— Although member participation is high in these groups, status consensus is made impossible, since any ascendant leader cannot function effectively in competition with the trainer. Similarly, perceived goal achievement is low in early sessions, since members perceive an exacerbation of group problems rather than an alleviation of them. It is only after defense mechanisms have been recognized and attitudes have changed that the trainer plays a more positive role and in so doing re-creates status consensus, raises perceived goal attainment with positive statements, and so increases member satisfaction. We suggest, therefore, that the trainer, by manipulating two important variables, reduces member satisfaction in the early stages of the group process. This satisfaction-reduction is used to motivate the search for a more meaningful means of construing the members' relationships with each other and with the trainer than those learned in childhood situations.

The third type of group is one of the most discussed groups in a natural setting, the formal organizational work group such as exists in many businesses. We have already discussed such groups, suggesting reasons why difficulties concerning status consensus are likely to affect member satisfaction adversely. We noted that for a considerable time this recurring problem has been coped with by such measures as: (i) legitimising occupancy of the high position by the recruitment to it of persons with unmistakable marks of success, such as degrees or former occupancy of other high-status positions; (ii) choosing individuals with high status in other spheres such as fame, social prestige, wealth, age; (iii) granting symbols of status such as titles, a superior office, a high salary, rituals of authority; and (iv) placing the occupant in a position where crucial information is available to him and not to others.

Member participation in formal organization groups is usually concerned with implementing decisions rather than making them, and is best understood in terms of the member's expectations of the amount and type of participation he ought to have. In regard to our third variable, we suggest an important factor which has been generally neglected. For whereas high goal attainment has always been sought and emphasized in formal organizations, frequently the importance of providing feedback to members has been ignored. Our review of the literature has suggested that it is not goal attainment per se which leads to increased member satisfaction but rather perception by members of the group's progress towards its goals. Where an organization is aiming to increase the satisfaction of its members, particular attention should be paid to the setting of realistically attainable short-term goals, and to the prompt non-perfunctory communication to members of progress toward and attainment of these goals.'

(1964: 99-112)

Roles of Members

One very instructive method of looking at the ways in which
members operate within groups is to examine the roles which
they occupy at different times within the group. In the section
on leaders (the leader being a member role of some significance),
it was noted that leadership acts tended to fall into two main
areas of behaviour, i.e. those directed toward achieving the goals
of the group — task-oriented, and those directed toward
smoothing relationships between members — socioemotionally-
oriented. Generally the roles of all members fall within one or
both of these categories. Benne and Sheats's category, which they
refer to as 'group building and maintenance roles', which are
mainly roles directed toward the perpetuation of the group *qua*
group, in most senses seems to be concerned with the emotional
problems of group members. Their individual category is an
extension of this socioemotional function but concerned
expressly with the individual member's problems of relating to
the group.

Obviously, within a group situation members will act in ways
which are designed to forward the task of the group, or to make
it easier for the group to work together or to ease their own
position in the group (or perhaps establish or maintain it).
Though Benne and Sheats give a large number of member roles,
not all of which are mutually exclusive, it is part of the technique
of a group worker to be able to recognize the group or individual
purpose of such acts and to encourage those which he sees as
necessary and forwarding the group; or to interpret them for the
purpose of creating enlightenment and enhanced awareness when
such a purpose is desirable.

Quite clearly there is a very close link between the recognition
of roles in this sense and the methods which have been devised
for recording the interaction of members during group sessions.
This is discussed in chapter 6. Also there is a close connection
between this kind of identification and the processes of intervention. As has already been suggested, roles which enhance
group movement in the required direction may be deliberately
encouraged and those which impede may well be extinguished by
lack of encouragement and hence by a diminution of member
satisfaction.

Role Conflict

Because each member of a social system plays many roles it follows that they may not all be compatible and conflict develops. Toby (1966) attempts to analyse the essential nature of such conflict in terms of legitimate claims and systems of priorities which in essence are techniques of role conflict avoidance.

Amongst the techniques discussed is 'etiquette' which is perhaps not such a surprising inclusion as might at first sight appear. All the techniques are based on a limited number of possibilities and the major ones are concerned with a non-recognition of the true value of one of the conflicting claims. Etiquette provides an avoidance technique of this nature by providing a usage for occasions which would inevitably be possible conflict situations. Group situations can provide an etiquette of their own which can be very puzzling to the new-comer if an initiation ceremony does not include knowledge of the basic behavioural patterns. Also the apparent lack of conventional behavioural procedures in some groups can be very disturbing to members whose lives are supported by an acceptance of codes of socially acceptable behaviour.

Role conflict is uncomfortable and though it is tolerated in many circumstances because it is seen as inevitable or necessary, when psychic discomfort increases beyond a given point some attempt will usually be made to restore a greater degree of comfort. For instance, conflict between personal demands and those of the group may occur. If this situation is continuous then the member's satisfaction in being a member will decline markedly and given that he has egress, the member may eventually leave in order to reduce the level of his discomfort. Of course, it is possible that a state of stalemate can ensue if only for a short period, where the pull in any of several directions is absolutely equal to any of the others, resulting in a period of complete indecision.

Toby writes about role definition referring to it as role segregation. This implies that potentially conflicting roles may be segregated by defining them in ways in which they cannot conflict because they cannot cover the same interests. Thus the group worker has a professional role as well as his role as an individual member of the group. Decisions made as a professional may be acceptable to the group which would be rejected if they were seen as emanating from the individual in a non-professional role. Frequently the professional role is not well enough defined, or is even rejected by the group worker and the resulting confusion stems from the lack of definition of the role he is playing at any given moment. This can be used of course in order to cause group members to face their own attitudes concerning the roles they see others playing, e.g. leadership roles.

Deindividuation

Festinger, Pepitone, and Newcomb (1952) are concerned with the phenomenon of 'deindividuation', i.e. the apparent way in which members of a group feel that they are no longer so easily identifiable as separate entities when functioning within the group. This leads to behaviour which seems different from their individually normal behaviour when away from the group. The authors postulate that, because the group makes possible the performance of behaviours of this kind, the group increases member satisfaction. In fact, their major theses are (1) that deindividuation does occur in groups and (2) that groups, where it does occur, are more attractive to members than groups where it does not occur.

> 'We would like to advance the theory that, under conditions where the member is not individuated in the group, there is likely to occur for the member a reduction of minor restraints against doing various things. In other words, many of the behaviours which the individual wants to perform but which are otherwise impossible to do because of the existence, within himself, of restraints, become possible under conditions of the de-individuation in a group.' (1952: 382-389)

In their summary the authors say:

> 'A group phenomenon which we have called de-individuation has been described and defined as a state of affairs in a group where members do not pay attention to other individuals qua individuals, and, correspondingly, the members do not feel they are being singled out by others. The theory was advanced

that such a state of affairs results in a reduction of minor restraints in the members and that, consequently, the members will be more free to indulge in behaviour from which they are usually restrained. It was further hypothesized that this is a satisfying state of affairs and its occurrence would tend to increase the attractiveness of the group. . .' (1952: 382-389)

This work has been quoted because it attempts to validate a well known factor of behaviour in groups. Much has been written about crowd behaviour relevant to this point:

'excitement begins to spread. As it does, members of the community or a portion of them, usually selected on a social class basis, begin to interact with one another in a direct highly emotional manner. Through gestures, tone of voice, and actual content of speech they heighten the emotional excitement of each participant. As the crowd begins to form, a universal feeling of anonymity, combined with the emergence of attitudes deeply buried in the personality, develops . . . Self-appointed leaders arise and channel the energies of the crowd in the direction it is already moving. The attention of the members is centered increasingly on a single object and purpose. At a certain pitch of emotional tension the crowd acts. It may continue to act for some time until the emotional level drops. The crowd then dissolves and self-awareness returns to its members.' (Wilson and Kolb, 1949: 307)

Given a strong emotional factor the release of self-restraint does not take very long to occur in such a crowd situation, but it must not be forgotten that the members of the crowd may not be strangers if, as in the item quoted above, the crowd was formed in a small community. If a group can be demonstrated to help deindividuation in a life of forty minutes as was the case in the experimental groups, it is reasonable to expect that a greater increase in this factor should take place over a long group life when a stronger sense of group support has been developed.

For the group practitioner this article offers some evidence that the 'deindividuation' effect can take place fairly soon after a group meets for the first time. This being so, it may be necessary to prepare for the effect which follows when self-awareness is restored and the group support withdrawn until the next meeting.

Some feelings of over-exposure and remorse may well be apparent.

Scapegoats and Newcomers

Of all the roles that group members may take on or have thrust upon them, that of scapegoat is perhaps most widely known. It is a term well used in every day conversation and stems from Tyndale's translation of the bible in 1530. Garland and Kolodny (1970) have collected together most of the available ideas about this phenomenon which can produce distressing situations in any kind of group.

Basically scapegoating is an 'off-loading' technique and the scapegoat selected to receive these attentions either has to accept because he has no apparent alternative, or he does so because this kind of attention satisfies his own needs. In either case this is not such an easy problem to cope with but when the two main bases of scapegoating are combined it becomes very difficult indeed because intervention is likely to decrease drastically the satisfactions of those involved.

Recognition of this phenomenon in a group presents little difficulty over a period of time because of its repetitive nature, the same person being made the centre of an attack at every opportunity. However, there is a little evidence to suggest that there may be several kinds of scapegoat.

Mann (1967) describes a sexual scapegoat; Berkowitz and Green (1962) discuss the factor of perceived difference in the scapegoat which draws dislike. Certainly scapegoats operate in the socioemotional sphere of group maintenance; by drawing bad feeling upon themselves, or having it placed there, they release energy for other purposes. Olmsted (1959) describes it as a 'leadership' role directed to group harmony (see following diagram) in the area of expressive activity.

The emotional consequences of continued scapegoating are however not all good, for the tendency may well develop for the group to maintain its existence at the cost of the suffering of one person. This is a denial of individual responsibility and groups designed for sensitization purposes have to cope with this neurotic adjustment, as with others, by a confrontation of those involved with their 'here and now' behaviour in order that

Table 7

	Social Structure ('inner situation' relationship among members)	Culture ('outer situation' relationship among ideas and values)
instrumental activity ——— task-oriented	(1) Dimension of social activity (a) the division of labour, staff function (b) the structure of authority line or guidance function Leader Roles (a) technical expert (b) executive	(2) Dimension of cultural symbols Knowledge – information Leader Roles (a) ideas man, analyst (b) synthesizer
expressive activity ——— group-oriented	(3) Dimension of social activity (a) network of affective ties (b) solidarity Leader Roles (a) best liked (b) harmonizer (joker, host roles, scape-goat)	(4) Dimension of cultural symbols Values Leader Roles (a) style-setter, artist (b) symbolic figure-head consensus creator (the 'crown')

Category (a) differentiation – centrifugal and specialized
(b) integration – centripetal and generalized

(Olmsted, 1959: 139)

progress can be made to more stable and mature methods of group and individual maintenance.

Garland and Kolodny concentrate on the classic and traditional form of scapegoat and scapegoater, but there are many indications that some people in a group are scapegoated because they are seen to be lagging behind the general progress of the group. Attacks on this kind of person (e.g. Mann's sexual scapegoat) serve to clarify for the group what kind of progress they have made and what kind of moves should be made next. This is almost entirely a group beneficial gambit and needs supportive handling rather than protective or restrictive, so that the group is not inhibited in its progress.

The authors offer a range of twelve methods of coping with the phenomenon of the scapegoat, varying from virtual surgery to elaborate attempts at enlightenment. But any kind of intervention (even non-intervention) needs to be based on a clear recognition of what is happening, not only that scapegoating is taking place, but what kind of scapegoating and at what level of intensity.

The Newcomer

The difficulties which can face a newcomer seeking to enter an established group are quite well known in our society. A new job, a new school, a new member of the family, are all familiar situations that pose problems of acceptance, assimilation, of adaptation and modifications of established patterns of behaviour.

Freud regarded the general distrust of strangers as being basically narcissistic in origin, i.e. love of oneself engendered self-satisfaction and the very strangeness of others was an implied criticism of one's self-assurance and tended to provoke hostility and aggression. In anthropological works 'the passing stranger' was frequently thought to be subjected to being sacrificed, because he was felt to possess magical powers. Contact with such strangers tended to be very stringently organized and many taboos hedged about his reception. He was regarded as a potential threat.

Some writers have seen the group reaction to the outsider as stemming from the basic organization of the family. In the small family group the arrival of a baby alters the total configuration of the family as a unit and generally the smaller the family the more the resulting change. Children learn responses to strangers as part of their development and these responses vary from fear at a very early age to some degree of ability to use acceptable social techniques in dealing with this situation later in life.

In most group situations there are accepted procedures for the admission of new members. Many of these are highly formalized and may in fact obscure their original meaning which was to ease the passage of the valued person from the state of non-member to that of member and also to exclude the unworthy. Such rituals of acceptance include periods of probation and assessment; reference to other respected opinion; the creation of bonds between the group and the prospective member and the establishment of the applicant's viability and worth.

Most human beings have been brought up in group situations and have therefore been faced with the need for acceptance all their lives. The need to belong may be accepted as being fundamental to every human being. This being so it follows that in order to meet this need man will continually attempt to join groups which appear to him to offer satisfaction, not only of his basic need to be accepted, but also of other needs which may or may not be constant. He tends thus to find himself more or less frequently in the role of newcomer in an established group. The problems of the role of 'newcomer' have not been studied extensively but what investigation there has been so far tends to indicate quite clearly the main factors involved in this situation. From the viewpoint of those who use 'groups' as a form of social treatment such knowledge could greatly facilitate the process of assimilation of the newcomer. It is therefore instructive to look at this problem both from the angle of the group and from that of the member attempting to join it and also to consider in what ways such understanding as may be created can be used.

Any group with a large membership turnover may be expected to have adopted procedures for the admission of new members and its stability is rarely affected by the advent of one new member with different ideas. Such groups tend to be large permanent institutions and admission, change, and departure are an everyday occurrence. In smaller groups with a small turnover, size is no longer a protecting factor. What begins to count in this situation are such factors as the experience of the group, its purpose, composition, and stage of development.

In a group which has been in existence a long time, the roles accepted and performed by each member may have become fixed and the life of the group become somewhat stagnant. The entry of a newcomer to a group of this nature will be difficult for there is little opportunity within it for personal development. The more rigid such a group has become, the more set and habitual its ways, the more likely it is to ensure that any newcomer is made aware that he is expected to accept the situation as it is or keep out.

This kind of situation is the result of the forces making for cohesion within the group. At different stages in any group's life these forces possess different strengths and consequently affect the introduction of a new member in different ways. For instance in the early stages of a group's life, what Foulkes and Anthony (1957) call the 'me' stage, the members are still strangers and their responses to the group situation are individual and based on previous attempts to cope with similar situations. At this stage new members are fairly easily accepted and equally easily others may leave. The shared experience of the group members is not significantly longer than the 'no shared' experience of the newcomer.

At a later stage the group has increased its shared experience, its members have struggled, argued, and worked together and produced a feeling of an 'encapsulated society'. Into this situation a newcomer will not be readily accepted and in fact the resentment of his intrusion, his obvious difference and strangeness may be sufficient for the members to combine to drive him away.

So far it has been assumed that the newcomer has made application to an existing group for membership and that this is the usual situation. However it is necessary to make a distinction between such an application when the newcomer is seen as a substitute for a previous member who has left and when he is an addition to the group without the loss of an original member.

In the first instance it is obvious that the newcomer will interact with the original members at a different rate from his predecessor and that he will thus disturb the balance of the group necessitating adjustments both on his part and on the part of the other members to restore equilibrium at a different level. In the second situation it is usual for the older members of the group to adjust to the newcomer and for a decrease in the interaction rate between individuals in the group to take place.

It is possible to adduce several possible occurrences in group behaviour when another member is added. Straightaway the number of possible relationships between members is increased though the time which each member then has for communicating with others is correspondingly decreased. An increasing number of members must feel threatened and inhibited by the addition of new members despite the fact that up to the point of operation of the law of diminishing returns the resources of the group will be increased — as for instance, the range of ideas, which must surely be increased. But against this must be placed the fact that the increase in numbers which brings about the increased production of ideas also will tend to create greater difficulty for the group to reach agreement about them.

Increases in group size (by the addition of a new member) can increase the satisfactions each member gets from his membership. Where the needs of members begin to correlate then the struggle for power within a group will tend to decline and become less necessary. With these and many other possible effects upon group life stemming from the addition of a new member it is obvious that such an addition needs to be carefully considered by any group when the situation arises.

Up to this point the move of the newcomer has been considered to be a voluntary one on his part, especially from the point of view of the group. The main difference that compulsion may have on the role of newcomer has not been fully investigated but it would seem to enhance most of the difficulties which occur in the voluntary situation because the element of attraction which is so relevant to ordinary group membership is missing.

The individual who becomes a new member in a group brings with him his previous experience of similar situations. Thus he may have become stereotyped into a limited number of roles which he will play irrespective of the group situation. The admission of such a person is bound to be fraught with difficulties, because a person's membership within a group provisionally depends upon his acceptance of the reference frame of that particular group. The group's norms are given him as a standard and he is expected to adhere to them.

As the stage of group development is a significant factor in the admission of a new member so too are the stages of acceptance of the newcomer by the group. These phases of entry can be seen to occupy four different levels. Thus at the beginning the newcomer attempts to interact with the others at the level of behaviour and feeling, he sees what is done and he is aware of what is felt. Second, he becomes aware of the rules of the group, the reasons for the way the group members behave, and feel. Third, he recognizes, accepts, and becomes willing to strive for, the aims which the group have set up, and finally he becomes identified with the members of the group as a whole.

When an individual enters a group he tends to seek for links through common experience and similarities. He observes what others do, does what he is asked to do, and attempts to make himself secure. He tends to select those who may be helpful as allies and to avoid those who can hurt him; he is orientated toward survival and tends to play safe.

Primarily he is following a pattern which he does not fully understand. At this stage he cannot really be aware of the meaning that this particular group places on any part of this pattern, nor, although he is able to feel with the group, is he aware of the significance of this feeling for the group. He is in a state of ignorance and only by adapting to the prevailing pattern can he begin to detect the local meanings of the parts of the pattern. In other words until he is able to say that he understands the way his fellow members think, and until he is able to point to successful shared experience with them he has not truly been assimilated.

Certain factors will however change this pattern of the stages of assimilation, the main influence being the worth or quality of the newcomer as seen by the group he wishes to join. If he is perceived as having status and great worth to the group, i.e. he has something which the group needs, e.g. knowledge or skill, then he will tend to be exempted from some of the stresses and strains which normally accompany assimilation. He will also tend to be excluded from real membership and subjected to being the focus of the group's expectations and hopes. Only when the group becomes aware of his underlying ordinariness can he become a member of the group and conflict and embarrassment will only develop if the new member does not relinquish his high status role when the need for it is passed.

If a new member is perceived as possessing a low status he will encounter the anxiety and hostility reserved for outsiders and his own feelings of possibly not measuring up to what may be expected of him will be reinforced.

In particular the person who becomes a group leader may be subjected to such stresses. The group worker is always the 'outsider' and until the group have tested him and found him worthy of their trust little significant interaction between them can take place. Where the group leader is not himself the newcomer then he may well be the only positive link the newcomer has with the group, and certainly more demands for co-ordination will be made by the group of the leader.

Finally some consideration should be given to ways in which the induction of a newcomer may be facilitated. This implies that some reduction of anticipatory anxiety both in the group and the member would be essential. The methods which have so far been identified are largely concerned with preparation. Thus the new member is instructed in the nature of the group he is about to enter and common links are sought and enhanced. Channels of communication are an important feature of this process and the advantages of the member and the group highlighted each to the other. The challenges and anxieties which are reactivated by the presence of the newcomer and which disturb the complacency of the group have to be dealt with in terms of explanation and understanding. Group activities that allow the entry of the newcomer without difficulty are obviously of value as indeed is the age-old process of the initiation ceremony, whether this be in the form of a test or an induction by an established member or group of members.

Whatever preparation can be made it is essential to understand that many people suffer in the role of the newcomer because of their need for acceptance and their awareness of the hurt of rejection. It is also a role which most people play many times in their lives.

Interpersonal Attraction

It has already been demonstrated that whether or not the members of a group like one another and the group as a whole has a great effect upon the level of satisfaction they derive from being a member and consequently upon their commitment to the group and its aims. Berkowitz and Green (1962) based their theory of why certain people in a group were selected as scapegoats upon the fact of fairly intense personal dislike, largely brought about by the perception of differences. So it is of great value to find an article, like Newcomb's (1965), which reviews much of the available material concerned with why people like one another and which attempts to show the common aspects of this material.

Elsewhere some attempt has been made to show that knowledge of the factors which enhance or diminish personal liking can be made the basis of intervention strategies designed to affect such things as acceptance by the group of a member or even the over-all performance of the group in pursuit of its aims.

It is interesting to note that the term 'social intervention', much favoured by group theorists, is dropped by Newcomb in favour of 'communicative behaviour' — 'because it calls attention to certain consequences that are characteristic to information exchange, but not of energy exchange, among symbol-using humans' (1965). Newcomb develops this into two propositions 1) that communicators tend to become more similar to each other even if only for a brief period and 2) attraction toward a communicator depends upon a perceived similarity of attitudes toward the object of communication.

For the group worker the conclusions drawn in this paper are important, particularly that interpersonal attraction develops and changes under orderly conditions and that certain factors give a reasonable chance of predicting such attraction. Such factors can therefore be used to enhance attraction between members under circumstances where this is desirable, e.g. the arrival of a new member in a group — the support of a member through a particularly difficult period. Conversely attraction may be decreased by reversing the procedure, e.g. demonstrating that different attitudes exist on important subjects between members who are aware largely only of their level of similarity of attitudes.

Interaction

'The essence of any interpersonal relationship is interaction. Two individuals may be said to have formed a relationship when on repeated occasions they are observed to interact. By interaction is meant, that they emit behaviour in each other's presence, they create products for each other, or they communicate with each other. In every case we would identify as an instance of interaction there is at least the possibility that actions of each person affect the others.'

'A group may be regarded as an open interaction system on which actions determine the structure of the system and successive interaction.'

(Thibaut and Kelley, 1959: 70)

The process of interaction which takes place between the members of a group is the crucial focal point of the study of group behaviour. Whatever study is made of groups is directly or indirectly concerned with the way the members of that group interact with each other and with what kind of factors influence that interaction and in what way and to what extent. In a wide sense interaction could be taken to mean all the actions of the members of a group, but this breadth of definition would be useless.

'Inter' action implies action 'between' persons and cannot be an isolated action which elicits no response. Thus a unit of interaction, i.e. the smallest possible piece of behaviour which can be so classified, must be composed of one action by A which is received by B who then responds. Bales and Slater (1955) put it this way:

'The description of the behaviour of an individual from the interactional point of view includes not only how he acts toward others (output), but also how others respond to him (input). For this reason the minimum of actions involved is two, the minimum number of acts is two (1 action and 1 reaction) and the minimum number of time periods in which interaction occurs is two.' (1955)

Stogdill (1959), also attempting to define the action/reaction nature of interaction, writes that interaction occurs when 'in a system composed of two members, A reacts to B and B reacts to A in such a manner that the response of each is a reaction to the behaviour of the other.' This he elaborates later to show that while reaction is a one way process, an interaction seen from the point of view of either of the participants presents an inverse appearance to the way it appears to the other. The interaction is common to both parties and exists only so long as action and reaction exist.

Practically every factor which can affect group behaviour can affect interaction. Important in this respect are the factors of individual personality, group factors like size, composition, task, position, style, status, structure etc., and also factors like the environment in which the group exists. In other words almost the whole of the rest of this book is concerned with the ways in which these factors influence interaction. At this point then it is only necessary to give such examples as may clarify the general concept of interaction and to look at attempts which have been made to record interaction in actual group situations. 'Interaction is not a characteristic of individuals, but individuals differ in their capacity or inclination to enter into interaction with other persons — some in pairs others with large groups — some interact better in some social situations than others'. (Stogdill, 1959: 18).

Thus individuals react differently because they are differently prepared. The visible signs of interaction are the behaviour patterns which occur in group situations. Hare (1962) indicates diagrammatically the elements of the interaction process by showing the personal elements of individual biological nature and personality on one side and the elements of the environment, culture, and role on the other.

Observable behaviour between group members can be seen to spring from previous preparation in similar situations plus an application of the personal situation in terms of available coping behaviour patterns. Hare (1962) sees the forms of this behaviour as two (i) communication patterns, and (ii) the interaction rate. Much more will be said about communication later, interaction rate is quite simply the intensity of the interaction process usually recorded as the number of certain behaviours, e.g. the number of times A spoke to B, B to C etc.

However most observers of interaction between group members also divide it up into other sections according to its content or purpose. Thus Hare has two main categories: behaviour which is orientated toward socioemotional problems and behaviour which is oriented toward the group task. Based on similar analyses, there have been several attempts to assess the part of the individual in the interaction process e.g. by recording

Figure 8. *Elements of Social Interaction*

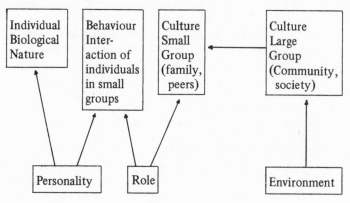

A paradigm for the analysis of interaction:

Form	Communication network	the channels of communication between members
	Interaction rate	the frequency of interaction [talk, time, number of contacts, etc.]
Content	Task Behaviour a) Observe b) Hypothesize c) Propose action	interaction directed toward the completion of individual group tasks
	Social Emotional Behaviour a) Control b) Affection	interaction directed primarily toward relationships

Each of the 'content' categories can be used at the level of personality [tendencies to act], behaviour and role [expectations for behaviour].   (Hare, 1962: 8; 11) output, i.e. communication or contact addressed to others, and input, i.e. communication or contact received from others. Bales (1950) produced the model shown in the diagram in the section on observing which shows the social-emotional and task-oriented areas divided into negative and positive and a further subclassification into six problem areas. Using this analysis and the recording sheet derived from it, it is possible to record the interaction of members of a group. However, all interaction is not observable. Straight recording of observable interaction is too simple and cannot allow for individual perception of cues at different levels from which they were intended. So the whole situation is complicated by individual values, past experience etc., and the relative impossibility of understanding accurately complex behavioural emissions. Zaleznik and Moment (1964: 27) writing about routine and predictability in social interaction say, 'A definition of the situation involves establishing the identity of the social setting in the minds of the participants. The identity evokes behavioural responses deemed appropriate to it . . . the participants can rely on routine, learned behaviour in the past to guide their interactional responses.' Thus any interaction between members of the group depends to a large extent upon the expectations of each individual in the interaction, which are in turn based upon the way he perceives the situation. He gives and receives cues and interprets both in terms of his definition of the situation.

Interaction tends to break down through ambiguity, i.e. when expectations of a given situation are not realized, when they are contradicted or disorientated. Tension created in this way usually forces some reassessment of the situation and the production of new and different responses.

Zaleznik and Moment point to the factors of 'selectivity' and 'content' in the interaction process. 'Members tend to interact with others who have a somewhat higher status and/or with whom they share values.' Thus interaction tends to have an upward bias in terms of the rank of the members involved or to follow the path of shared values and in this sense interaction may be said to have a selective bias. The member who has the highest status 'tends to direct his interaction more to the group as a whole than to individuals'.

Not only is there a relationship between the amount of

Figure 9

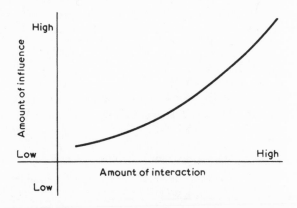

(Zaleznik and Moment, 1964: 72)

interaction and status or influence but also status tends to dictate the choice of members with whom a given individual will interact most frequently.

Stogdill points to the fact that individual difference affects the frequency of interaction. He calls 'emotional expansiveness' that factor which accounts for individual difference in 'the number of persons they characteristically choose as interaction partners' and 'social expansiveness' that factor which causes individuals to be different in 'the number they contact as interaction partners'.

Israel (1956) makes the point that group structure can affect the quality of the more generally assumed aspects of interaction. Where the structure of a group is co-operative the action of any individual which can be seen to be helping the group to achieve its goal is likely to be highly valued and to produce friendly attitudes in the group. The frequency of interaction in such a group will increase, especially if every member is able to originate interaction, providing only that such interaction causes movement toward the group goal. If it does not provide such a movement then those who initiate such kinds of interaction will tend to decrease the quantity of goodwill or liking they would otherwise receive.

In groups with a competitive structure interaction which moves the group towards the goal 'may clearly indicate who is more likely to achieve the goal'. Depending on how important the goal is to the others, such a person will tend to incur dislike. Thus the same kind of interaction in each group would produce dissimilar results because the style of each group is different.

The relationship of interaction and interpersonal liking is usually considered to be reciprocal but Cartwright and Zander indicate that 'There is some evidence that interaction which is unpleasant will cause people not to like one another better.' (1953: 80). A fact which is well enough established in common experience.

Jackson (1953) lists the functions of interaction as follows:

(1) to provide individual members with social reality concerning others' expectations and evaluations
(2) to reinforce approved behaviour and extinguish disapproval
(3) to attract or repel persons from membership
(4) to maintain the quality of the social system by drawing highly valued members into centrality and by making peripheral, or repelling, the small contributor.

REFERENCES

Bales, R.F. (1950) *Interaction Process Analysis.* Reading, Mass.: Addison Wesley.

Bales, R.F. and Slater, P.E. (1955) Role Differentiation in Small Decision-Making Groups. In T. Parson (ed.) *The Family, Socialization and Interaction Process.* Glencoe, Ill.: Free Press.

Benne, K.D. and Sheats, P. The Functional Roles of Group Members. In J.W. Orton (ed.) *Readings on Group-work.* Selected Academic Readings.

Berkowitz, L. and Green, J.W. (1962) The Stimulus Qualities of the Scapegoat. *Journal of Abnormal and Social Psychology* **64**: 293-301.

Cartwright, D. and Zander, A. (1953) *Group Dynamics, Research and Theory.* London: Tavistock.

Festinger, L. Pepitone, A. and Newcomb, T.M. (1952) Some Consequences of Deindividuation in a Group. *Journal of Abnormal and Social Psychology* **47**: 382-9.

Foulkes and Anthony (1957) *Group Psychotherapy.* Harmondsworth: Penguin.

Garland, J.A. and Kolodny, R.L. (1970) Characteristics and Resolution of Scapegoating. In S. Bernstein (ed.) *Further Explorations in Groupwork.* Boston Univ. School of Social Work.

Hare, A.P. (1962) *Handbook of Small Group Research.* N.Y.: Free Press.

Heslin, R. and Dunphy, D. Three Dimensions of Member Satisfaction in Small Groups. *Human Relations* **19**: 94-112.

Israel, J. (1956) *Self-Evaluation and Rejection in Groups.* Uppsala: Almaquist and Wiksell.

Jackson, J.M. (1953) Reference Group Processes in a Formal Organisation. D. Cartwright and A. Zander (eds.) *Group Dynamics.* London: Tavistock.

Mann, R.D. (1967) *Interpersonal Styles and Group Development* N.Y.: John Wiley.

McGrath, J.E. and Altman, I. (1966) *Small Group Research: a synthesis and critique of the field.* N.Y.: Holt, Rinehart and Winston.

Newcomb, T.M. (1965) The Prediction of Interpersonal Atrraction. *American Psychologist*

Northen, H. (1969) *Social Work with Groups.* Boulder, Col.: Col. U.P.

Parsons, T. and Bales, R.F. (eds) (1955) *Family Socialization and Interaction Process.* Glencoe, Illinois: Free Press.

Olmsted, M.S. (1959) *The Small Group.* N.Y.: Random House.

Stogdill, R.M. (1959) *Individual Behaviour and Group Achievement.* N.Y.: O.U.P.

Thibaut, J.W. and Kelley, H.H. (1959) *Social Psychology of Groups.* N.Y.: John Wiley.

Toby, J. (1966) Some Variables in Role Conflict Analysis. In C.W. Backman and P.F. Secord (eds.) *Problems in Social Psychology.* N.Y.: McGraw-Hill.

Wilson, L. and Kolb, W.L. (1949) *Sociological Analysis.* N.Y.: Harcourt Brace.

A. Zaleznik and D. Moment (1964) *Dynamics of Interpersonal Behaviour.* N.Y.: John Wiley.

9

Social climate, threat and trust

'An atmosphere of acceptance and permissiveness is of basic importance for all aspects of group guidance. By acceptance is meant that each individual will be accorded respect and a status of belonging to a cohesive we-group, no matter what his personal characteristics or problems may be at the moment. If behaviour is objectionable or disruptive, a distinction will be made between the individual and the unacceptable behaviour. Permissiveness denotes freedom to express any ideas or feelings for consideration by the group with the awareness that all members will attempt to understand and to continue to accept each other as respected individuals in spite of disagreement with, or disapproval of, ideas or behaviour.' (M.E. Bennet, 1963: 87)

A group which is most effective in problem-solving is one in which the atmosphere lends itself to problem-solving and where the group is large enough to have sufficient experience to offer and yet is small enough to permit the maximum amount of participation and the minimum of threat.

The atmosphere of a group may be defined as the general psychological or emotional state of the group at a given moment. If this atmosphere persists generally through the life of a group, then this is described as the group's climate. Climate may be one of indecision, anxiety, insecurity, happiness, etc. Climate has a great effect upon the members of a group in that they will tend to behave according to the way they perceive the prevailing atmosphere. The expectations of members of what is about to occur within a group will also be very important in determining the climate. For example, in the classic experiment on authority and leadership, autocratic leaders tended to produce aggressive or apathetic climates, with rebellious or dependent behaviour patterns on the part of the members, and low capacity amongst these members for initiating any new group action. Laissez-faire leaders produced more discontent, hostility, and certainly less friendliness. Democratic leaders tended to produce a friendly atmosphere.

A group's atmosphere tends to range somewhere between 'defensive' and 'accepting'. A defensive atmosphere tends to make members unable to communicate freely, there is a strong disinclination to disagree with other members, or to express ideas and feelings which could be seen as going in a different direction to that of the group. Where the atmosphere in a group is tightly controlled, punitive, and with rigid rules, the behaviour of the group will tend to become conforming, dependent, or occasionally apathetic. On the other hand, an accepting atmosphere will induce members to listen, to understand and to trust. Such a group will usually develop a greater sense of belonging, of working together, and with more helping relations among the members.

Gibb (1970) relates defensiveness to perceived threat, or anticipated threat. The challenge of improving communications thus becomes one of behaving in ways that reduce threat. This in turn implies the building of suitable socioemotional climates.

Gibb isolated two contrasting climates and six categories of behaviour that are characteristic of each of them:

1) Defensive climates tend to be induced by
    a) evaluation
    b) control
    c) strategy
    d) neutrality
    e) superiority
    f) certainty

2) Supportive climates tend to be induced by
   a) description
   b) problem orientations
   c) spontaneity
   d) empathy
   e) equality
   f) provisionalism

Gibb stresses the tendency of these two categories of behaviour to increase and reduce defensiveness, respectively, with individual reactions specifically depending on the level of personal defensiveness and the climate of interpersonal or group relations within which these behaviours occur. 'Reduced defensiveness permits receivers to "become better able to concentrate upon the structure, the content and the cognitive meanings of the message". The significance of climate can be established from another perspective. Not only do defensive communicators send off notable value, motive and affect cues, but defensive recipients also distort what they perceive' (1970: 64-65).

When considering the creation of equality and the reduction of threat in a group, the problem is to be able to analyse the factors which inhibit group interaction and those which faclitate it. In general, anything which produces threat or feelings of inadequacy will tend to reduce both the pleasure members get from the group and the productivity. Non-verbal communications play a large part in this particular respect. Thus obvious indications of power, separateness, status, all serve to indicate that, whatever may be being said at that particular moment, that equality is not present. Alternatively, non-verbal communications can equally well suggest feelings of equality. As for instance by the conscious use of such things as outgoing warmth, the use of acceptable names, informality, and permissiveness.

Most people feel some insecurity or uncertainty in groups because they are concerned about what other people will think of them. Also groups have developed a mythology of their own, and this tends to produce ideas in the uninitiated which are usually significantly out of proportion to what actually occurs. A large group has proportionately more individuals in it who are liable to be strangers and whose reactions may be difficult to judge. In threatening situations when people feel insecure, defensive mechanisms tend to be used. Everyone needs to be accepted and to be approved of by others in order to generate a sense of being recognized as an individual and to become secure. In circumstances where people feel that they are insecure, then the classic defensive mechanisms may arise, as for instance projection, rationalization, withdrawal.

Feelings of inadequacy or inferiority within a group may show in many ways. Any undue sensitivity to criticism is one very obvious indicator. Another may well be a strong tendency to criticize others. This is the search for security by disparaging others. Usually these kinds of feeling are accentuated when the problem a group is facing produces quite considerable difficulties or when stress conditions of one sort or another prevail.

An atmosphere of openness and trust within the group can decrease these feelings. Sensitivity to the needs of others within the group becomes a very important factor. When members are aware that trust and sincerity exist they will feel safe enough to be able to work with the group. This presupposes a fine adjustment between the task and purpose of the group and the needs of the individuals within it. Any individual attempting to satisfy his own needs and paying little attention to the needs of others will generally generate resentment and certainly, if not rejected from the group, will decrease the co-operation within it and increase the possible tension.

Obviously, at the beginning of any group the people in it are most concerned with the problem of relating one to another. Each individual member is producing behaviour which is largely governed by his perception of what is around about him – for instance, whether the group appears to be accepting him or not, or his apparent ability to be able to influence other members. Our cultural conditioning tends to preclude complete frankness and candid comment. Young children before they learn that this kind of behaviour is not allowed are given to making devastating remarks in public. It is therefore very difficult to be open about ourselves because we are constantly aware of our need to be liked, to be thought well of. Yet for a group to work effectively and in harmony it is necessary for the members of a group to have fairly accurate perceptions of each other.

If the group worker is faced with the dilemma of people attempting to reduce their own personal feelings of unease and knowing that in the long run the only way the group will work effectively is for group members to have developed a trust of each other, then the development of trust and the ability to work has to be formed over a period of time.

> I was angry with my friend,
> I told my wrath
> My wrath did end.
> I was angry with my foe
> I told it not
> My wrath did grow.
>
> William Blake.

Trust

'The sense of trust. This is a development of the very early months and years of life and grows out of the basic satisfactions of experiencing love and affection, of being an inseparable part of a family group, no matter what one does, and of knowing or feeling that wants will be met by others or can be met by oneself. It is perhaps the foundation of faith in others, in self, and in the goodness of life. Children who fail to develop this sense of trust may go through life unhappily disturbed about their place in life, feeling unloved and unable to love and lacking any faith in their fellow men or in themselves. Erikson says (*Childhood and Society*): "For most infants . . . a sense of trust is not difficult to come by. It is the most important element in the personality. It emerges at the most vulnerable period of a child's life, yet it is least likely to suffer harm, perhaps because both nature and culture work towards making mothers most maternal at that time." '

(M.E. Bennet, 1963: 88-9).

'In each new situation an individual faces, to some extent, renewal of the basic conflict of this sense of trust versus distrust and the need for synthesis of these polarities. The extent to which he has achieved a basic sense of trust influences the amount and duration of uncertainty and anxiety that is typical of encounters with the new situations. Each new experience offers some occasion for mistrust until the unknown becomes familiar. Until members can come to trust the people involved and the situation, they cannot participate in an interdependent relationship with others. The social worker develops by conveying, through his own attitudes and behaviour, the quality of acceptance, empathy and objectivity that are components of the professional relationship. He helps members to relate to him and each other through the many small courtesies that indicate interest in one's comfort and that acquaint members with each other, . . With the necessary amount of support and direction from the worker, members of the group who have a healthy sense of trust will move rather quickly into fuller exploration of the potentials and demands in the group experience . . .

Many persons lack a basic sense of trust in others and in their ability to cope with situations. For some, the symptoms will be withdrawal and fearful responses to efforts to engage their participation . . .

An informal atmosphere is usually conducive to development of trust in the worker as well as to the development of relationships among members . . .

Mutual trust will be developed between the worker and the group as varied situations occur that are of concern to the members, and as the worker deals with these in the person's best interests without violating the community's interest.' (Northen, 1969: 120-124).

Both these quotations emphasize certain points about the factor of trust which may be summarized as follows:
1) The degree and quality of trust is created by the maturational process and confirmed or otherwise by experience.
2) Groups do not work well when members do not trust each other.
3) The group worker can engender trust by acting as a role model for the members.

It is pertinent at this point to state that it is the practitioner's business to create trust. This can only be done by putting himself at risk. He must initiate, he must move towards others, he must expose himself to rebuff and hurt before others will move towards him. He is the conscious agent of group progress. He knows what is involved and has therefore the duty and responsibility of risking himself to show others the way.

Informality certainly does enhance contact and therefore trust, but informality may be inappropriate and engender hostility and suspicion and anxiety. Thus, informality needs careful adjustment, not only to various groups, but to the different stages of any one group's existence. Some degree of structure is always necessary for some people who would be bewildered and lost if they could not perceive some form — some order.

Gee and Kemp in the extract quoted below discovered that their approach had to be modified because the climate that a 'permissive' line engendered amongst the adolescent members of the group was fraught with anxiety and tension.

Working Towards a Method

'Although we had seen adolescents individually, neither of us had had previous experience of working with groups of adolescents. Our experience of group work had been with adults only. Thus to begin with we tried to lead the adolescent group as if they were adults and adopted the so-called orthodox approach in that we were non-directive and very task orientated. It soon became obvious that this was a mistake. Instead of talking between themselves like groups of adults, they said very little and spent most of the time sitting in silence. The long silences created a great deal of tension which was aggravated by our anxiety and we showed this by making occasional negative comments about the silence. Looking back it seems that we were afraid of being in any way directive because we feared that we might become over-involved. At that time we thought that being good therapists meant that for most of the time we should act like silent screens waiting for projections that we could interpret back. Thus these silences were experienced by us as frustrating our wish to be good therapists and the resulting anxiety led us into becoming hostile. Here is an example of how this hostitlity was expressed and its effect on the group:

At the beginning of this particular session there had been a long silence. Three of the members then had a short conversation, which was followed by another silence. This was broken by two of the female members whispering to each other. Until then neither of us had spoken, but not being able to contain our anger any longer one of us said:

"The behaviour so far this evening seems to have been aimed at destroying the group. First of all there was a long silence; then three people had a conversation which by its nature excluded the other three members of the group; this was followed by another silence, and then two people started whispering, which excluded the rest of us". After a short silence one of the female members said: "It's impossible to hold an intelligent conversation in the group which includes C. and R. because they are so backward".

This example seems to show mainly two things: Firstly, our lack of tolerance of their not behaving like adults, which led us into treating them like naughty children. Secondly, it shows that as a result of our persecuting them they then felt worthless and this was defended against by the creation of scapegoats who were, likewise, referred to as being worthless.

The need to create a better atmosphere was therefore obvious, and so slowly we were forced to realise that our preconceived ideas were no good. It was evident that we were not helping the adolescents and this was related to the fact, as we now can see, that we did not fully appreciate how fragile the adolescent is. In the process of learning this we found it all too easy to try to present them with answers or to push them into looking for answers to their many problems. This we found only underlined their feelings of worthlessness and reinforced their fantasies of the leaders being omnipotent. We were therefore faced with the problem of how to enable the adolescents to feel safe. It is well known that for effective treatment to take place the level of anxiety must not be too high nor too low. In the adolescent group the anxiety level was far too high.

How we Learned to Deal with the Anxiety Level
After a good deal of trial and error, we have found three ways of dealing with the problem of too much anxiety. Firstly, by being more directive. For some time now the groups have followed a pattern which we have found very helpful. On entering the room we make some friendly comments, and these are often followed by a very short silence which is usually broken by one of them bringing up a problem. If the silence is not broken in this way we now have no hesitation in

breaking it ourselves by asking one of them a question, which is often related to something that has been said the previous week. Once a problem has been verbalised we then invite comments from the others and in this way interaction between them develops. This we have found decreases the level of anxiety and enables the members to make more contributions, which, in turn, gives us more confidence. We now find that apart from being able to discuss individual problems, we are also able to see underlying group themes.

Secondly, we found it helpful on some occasions to explain to the adolescents, in everyday terms, some of the unconscious psychic-mechanisms, like projection or transference, as they occurred in treatment. This seems to reduce emotional intensity which is valuable for our adolescents as they are overwhelmed by their emotions most of the time.

Thirdly, anxiety was reduced by allowing some defensive attitudes and solutions to group problems. For example, in one group the members talked about the difficulties of making friends outside the group. One adolescent said that, "The trouble with having friends is that they restrict you in what you can do; whereas if you're on your own you can do what you like". This particular topic lasted for about twenty minutes, and although it was obvious to us after about five minutes that they were avoiding talking about their feelings towards each other (or doing so only indirectly), we remained silent. Eventually, however, we made a comment which enabled the members to look at their difficulties in trusting and sharing. We found, on the other hand, that if we made interpretations as soon as we became aware of the defence then this would freeze the members and they would not then be able to look at their feelings. We are aware that this is true for groups of adults, but we found that with adolescents it is necessary to wait much longer. It will also be realised that by asking direct questions we are actually providing them with defences. It is relevant to mention here that although our views are not yet clear we also feel that bringing adolescents together in a heterosexual group is probably not wise. Our adolescents all have difficulties with their sex identity, and forcing them to come face to face with the opposite sex seems premature for all of them. This is particularly so for the males.

Without exception all the females who have come to the
group have previously had sexual intercourse; whereas only
one of the male members has had intercourse. It is therefore
not surprising that the males should feel threatened in such a
group.' (1969: 12-16)

One final point of great significance in the consideration of
threat and trust needs to be made and that is the influence of
group development. Schutz (1958) put forward a very simple
formula as an aid to understanding this very important process.

$$\text{I.C.A.} \qquad [\text{I.C.A.}]^n \qquad \dots \text{A.C.I.}$$
I = Inclusion   C = Control   A = Affection   n = number of occasions

This formula states that people newly arrived in a group are
concerned with the problems of inclusion, e.g. how they will be
received, how far they want to go and so on. Here the sense of
threat will be great because unfamiliarity breeds insecurity and
the use of defences and previously successful behaviour used in
similar circumstances.

When the group moves past this stage it becomes concerned
with the problems of control, e.g. who possesses power? how
much? and how is it going to be used? Once again, although some
trust may well be developing, the struggle for power may pose
some considerable threat to some members, particularly if
conflict with the apparently established authority ensues.

Third, the group starts to establish bonds of liking based upon
shared experience and it is during this stage that trust develops
and the group becomes able to work as a group and not, as
previously, as isolated individuals or small subgroups.

Schutz indicates by his formula that this process is repeated
throughout the life of the group, usually when the group as a
whole is faced with some threat. At each repetition of the three
steps a healthy group emerges with a greater cohesion and an
improved working ability.

Finally, when the group has achieved its task, then the process
of winding down takes place and the formula goes into reverse.
Members renew affectionate contacts outside the group which
take on a greater significance than those inside, though these may
be continued on a new basis of friendship. Then members
relinquish control and finally dissolve their membership and
become excluded.

During this period there tends to be a restatement of some of the feelings of threat and also there is a decline in the element of trust. Change and the necessity of meeting the unknown recreates some of the problems of insecurity and uncertainty. Hopefully, members have learnt better methods of coping with these manifestations during the life of the group.

Most of the threat/trust problems which emerge in this process can be readily coped with when recognized. But they can also be distorted to destructive levels by insensitive forcing of the developmental rate of the group. Forcing a group to be too task-oriented before it has had time to consolidate its 'groupness' not only increases threat and retards the development of trust, but also delays and may destroy the group's ability ever to work together.

REFERENCES

Bennett, M.E. (1963) *Guidance and Counselling in Groups.* N.Y.: McGraw-Hill.

Gee, H. and Kemp, P. (1969) Starting an Adolescent Group: Some Anxieties and Solutions. *British Journal of Psychiatric Social Work* **10**(1): 12-16.

Gibbs, J.R. (1970) Defensive Communication. In R.T. Golembiewski and A. Blumberg (eds.) *Sensitivity Training and Laboratory Approach.* Illinois: F.E. Peacock.

Northen, H. (1969) *Social Work with Groups.* N.Y.: Columbia Univ. Press.

Schutz, W.C. (1958) *F.I.R.O. A Three-Dimensional Theory of Interpersonal Orientations.* N.Y.: Holt, Rinehart and Winston.

10

Termination

Here is my journey's end, here is my butt
And very sea-mark of my utmost sail.

Othello.

The termination of a group is part of its developmental sequence.
In the last section the simple formulation of Schutz was used to
show how a group had to work through the problems posed by
inclusion, control, and affection to the point at which it was able
to devote the maximum available effort to the essential purpose
of the group. The last section of Schutz's formula can be said to
show how a group, having achieved its task, or as much as may
be possible under the circumstances, comes to the point at which
it must cease to exist.

Not all groups die. Open groups in which the membership is
constantly changing may become institutions in the sense that a
corporate identity exists irrespective of the presence of any given
members. Thus, although old members leave and new members
arrive, there is a block somewhere in the middle which maintains
the group norms, has shared a considerable amount of experience
and thus ensures that the group's traditions will be carried on.

Once more the idea of preparation becomes of paramount importance. In the contract negotiated between the members of a group and its leader, therapist, or convenor, there is usually some period of time specified for which the group will exist. Thus from the moment of its inception a group is aware of its demise. 'The closing of a group should therefore be discussed well in advance so that feeling can be expressed – for example, by staying away' (McCullough and Ely, 1969:11).

What really matters is that the end of the group shall have been foreseen and planned for in such a way that the termination is seen as an integral part of the total group process. Barring accidents and other problems that cause the group to dissolve before task completion is achieved, groups which exist for a distinct and definable purpose should close when that purpose has been reached.

In effect the process of termination is a running down of a structure which hopefully is no longer necessary. For example, if the group has been educationally oriented, then the information has been absorbed and integrated; if the group was supportive, then adaptive behaviour has been upheld and the stress situation passed; if the group was created to change patterns of behaviour, attitudes, etc., then this modification has taken place as far as is possible under the cirumstances.

Solomon writing about terminating a group in an adult outpatient clinic says:

"The key to these procedures is the necessity for the group members to perceive termination as a symbol of growth than of loss. In many ways these procedures are similar to those aimed at developing and maintaining group cohesion. For example, group cohesion is fostered when the worker reassures the group that the group experience can help individual members learn to cope more effectively with their problems; that is, he expresses faith in the group's ability to achieve its purpose. On the other hand, separation from the group is made easier when the worker reassures the group that it is possible to take what has been learned in the group and continue to apply it in everyday social relations; he thereby expresses faith that the group's purpose has been achieved.' (1968)

Obviously this is far too simplistic, the expression of faith on the part of the worker can only have the kind of effect Solomon writes about if an almost total dependency of group members upon their leader exists. However, there is nothing wrong with a belief which squares with the observable facts of the group process, and the expression of such a belief can only be beneficial.

In a very simple way most groups may be said to be designed to come to an end. That is, the main purpose is to achieve some increments in the ability to cope of all the members. This being so, as Northen says 'The final phase is one during which the efforts of the social worker are directed mainly toward helping the members to stabilize the gains they have made and to prepare them for termination' (1969: 223).

It is easy to say that termination is based upon assessment, but difficult to achieve. Unless evaluations have been made of the progress of the group, and unless there was some kind of baseline at the group's inception, then assessment of progress becomes a matter of inspired or uninspired guesswork. Northen offers four possible assessments and decisions:

1) that there has been sufficient progress toward the achievement of the group's goals and there is potential for further development – the group should continue provided resources are still available;
2) that there has been sufficient progress but the potential for individual development and consolidation can take place without social work help – the group should be discontinued;
3) that there has been little progress – the group should continue providing there appears to be potential for change;
4) that there has been little progress with little or no potential for change – the group should be discontinued.

These 'planned' terminations arise as part of the continuous assessment of the group's progress by the practitioner. However, 'natural' causes also terminate a group, e.g.:

i) members leave the area
ii) members change their interests or their work
iii) members become ill

Changes within the organization in which the group is held may cause it to dissolve; low performance and achievement levels, the loss of leader even temporarily may be equally damaging. In all cases of natural termination and of the more unsatisfactory reasons of planned termination, the essential reason for the existence of the group has not been met. It is advisable that great care should be taken to ensure that alternative support systems should be provided for those group members who may well require help.

Granted that assessment has revealed the necessity of terminating the group then it becomes necessary to negotiate a contract of termination allowing sufficient time for readjustment to take place. The goal now becomes the dissolution of the group and the consolidation of all that has been gained in preparation for use outside it.

Many writers have discussed the reactions of group members to the introduction of the idea of termination and there is a great degree of similarity between their formulations which would seem to indicate that observable patterns of behaviour are fairly consistent. It is, however, difficult to judge how this similarity is maintained. Are all the groups informed of the time limit at the outset? How does this affect their subsequent behaviour? How does understanding of the developmental sequence of a group affect the approach to ending?

Hartford (1972) offers three stages in termination:
1) the period of preparation for ending
2) the termination itself
3) the plan for follow-up, if any.

This simple formula stresses preparation and follow-up if necessary. Too many groups are easily started, run by virtue of their own momentum, and die leaving a considerable feeling of 'let-down' among some members. Indeed, evidence is accruing to indicate that the more intensive the commitment of the members to the group sessions, then the more necessary is a well-planned and executed 'cooling-down' period.

During the preparation for the termination and the ending itself, the leader again assumes some of the responsibility he possessed in the opening stages. His was the responsibility for creating the group in the first instance, and however much the group has learned about its own processes in the meantime, his is the overall responsibility to ensure that the dispensing with the group's services is accomplished as effectively as possible and to the maximum possible benefit of each member.

'When a group is ready to disband, the conductor decides the date for termination and keeps the group at work through this period of dissolution. As already stated, all members of a closed group optimally end treatment together' (Walton, 1971:27).

Foulkes and Anthony suggest that termination should be gradual to allow the opportunity for 'working through' the change. Referring to analytic treatment groups they also quote the fact that a group ending causes members to reflect on the inevitability of death. The authors say that if a time for termination has been set early in the group, this will affect member behaviour at all stages. They continue:

'When confronted with the end, the group invariably finds many good and logical reasons for continuing, and these must be carefully analysed. They may resuscitate some of their forgotten symptoms or produce a few new ones. Their earlier dependency on the conductor may reaffirm itself as a transient phenomenon.

The conductor is himself a little more active than he was during the intermediate stage, and his activity is directed towards returning his patients back to normal life without any props.' (1957: 168-9)

Foulkes and Anthony point out that one great advantage of the group over an individual treatment situation is that it is nearer to real life. 'The transition is therefore smoother, and read-justment to reality and its demands easier. "Life outside" is not so different from the "miniature" society of group analysis, and in spirit every group is an open one - open to the "free ocean of life" outside.'

The rarefied atmosphere of group analysis has little in common with the groups run by most group workers, but it is very significant that the problems of terminating a group are so very similar in all cases. Given a lesser degree of personal commitment the 'separation' pangs are reduced, but without doubt they exist as does the easier transition referred to as existing in the group situation.

Richardson describes the ending of some 'education' groups in a very similar way:

'In several groups there were mocking references to Old Boys' Reunions with the recognition of the futility and unreality of such gatherings. In one there was a move to by-pass the reality of the ending by having a party, followed by a decision to abandon this false ending and face the real one. There was death imagery and the reference to "funeral rites", sometimes following ironically the imagery of the quickening and the birth that had so recently, it seemed, preceded these rites. There was the man who shocked some of the other members of his group by saying that when one mourns the death of a loved person, one is aware, paradoxically, of a new sense of freedom and release. In one group there was a fantasy about a remote island or castle to which the group might escape in order to preserve itself, in another fantasy about the sudden collapse of a bridge, that would save the group the pain of going on walking across it, knowing that it must ultimately face its own ending.' (1967: 114-15)

As noted earlier Northen mentions the fact of members leaving a group which continues to exist and in fact she offered material about groups closing for other reasons than achievement.

McLennan and Felsenfeld referring to groups of adolescents list four major reactions to separation:

1) the group attempts to ignore the fact;
2) they relive their shared experience;
3) they plan to meet again (reunion);
4) they try to finish all their business, withdraw interest, loosen ties, or express depression and anger.

There arises in this context the idea of partial termination, that is when the group is 'open' rather than 'closed'. An 'on going' group adds and loses members through a long life and the key issue becomes not so much one of total change but of the separation of individuals from a group which will continue to exist after their departure. The other end of this process, the addition of new members, has already been discussed.

McLennan and Felsenfeld write, 'If some members are going to terminate and others continue, there will be feelings stimulated on both sides. Members who are leaving may feel relieved, guilty, and anxious about their future, all at the same time. Those who are remaining may feel abandoned, angry that they have done less well' (1968: 108-9).

Quite obviously individual termination can cause many problems though there may be the advantage that open groups rarely develop the intensity of commitment of closed groups.

Finally in order to ensure that termination is clearly seen as part of the life of a group, a developmental sequence is given below with the final sequence expanded in greater detail.

Stage (1) Reaffiliation — approach avoidance

(2) Power and control

    a) rebellion and autonomy

    b) permission and the normative crisis

    c) protection and support

(3) Intimacy

(4) Differentiation

Garland, Jones, and Kolodny (1965) call the fifth stage of their developmental sequence of groups — 'separation'. They list the reactions to 'separation' as follows:

(5) Separation

    a) Denial

        1) simple denial — that ending was ever mentioned

        2) clustering — banding tighter together for protection

    b) Regression

        1) simple disorganized regression — sliding backward

        2) regressive fugue — desire to begin all over again

    c) 'We still need the club'

    d) Recapitulation

        1) re-enactment — repetition of early behaviours

        2) review — conscious reminiscing

    e) Evaluation — positive recapitulation

    f) Flight

        1) nihilistic flight — distinctive reaction to separation

        2) positive flight — positive 'weaning' moves

Bearing in mind that no developmental sequence is a straight line development, that there are cyclic and regressive effects, this fifth sequence seems to sum up most of what may occur in the termination of a group. Some of these problems are illustrated in the following extract from Brown and Smith:

Termination

'Working towards termination of the group was a special problem for us. When the group changed from a close, short-term group to a more open extended group, it was decided to run it in accordance with the school year. However, the leaders themselves were indefinite about whether the group would be ending or simply breaking for the school holidays. Mothers wanted to know quite early on if a group would be available in the new school year. Because of our uncertainty about this, the issue remained unresolved until close to the holiday period. The resulting problems became gradually more obvious and we realised that a clear decision had to be made. In spite of deciding to end the group and of communicating this about six sessions before the end, the mothers remained uncertain about the future and could not really accept that the group was ending. At the last session mothers exchanged addresses and made tentative plans to meet in the future. In these circumstances we were unable to be as helpful as we might have been in using termination as an experience of separation (certainly of particular importance to mothers of handicapped children).

In considering the usefulness of the group, mothers frequently mentioned how refreshing it was to have their own discussion. In spite of our initial explanation about the structure of the group and its open-ended content, the mothers came expecting a structured programme with speakers. Expectationss were based on past experience of more formal meetings and the response to this kind of group gives important clues as to structuring other services for these parents. The content of discussion in such a group becomes very broad indeed; the leaders must be prepared to discuss marital relationships, problems of normal siblings, or indeed all that it means to be a person in a community. In belonging to the group the mothers were integrated into a unit larger than that of the nuclear family. Because of the openness of this group the mothers had an opportunity to experience what mothers of normal children take for granted — occasion for expressing the satisfactions of motherhood, and talking about little ways in which their child had progressed. This is important because in their usual daily contacts their child is the difficult one, the one to be pited.' (1972: 17)

The evaluation of this group shows clearly the problems of 'expectations' which was caused by no real contract having been made in the first instance. But without doubt Brown and Smith were able to use the recapitulation drive of these final sessions both to provide learning for themselves and for their members.

REFERENCES

Brown, L.K. and Smith, J. (1972) Groups for Mothers. *Social Work Today* **3** (10): 17.

Foulkes, S.H. and Anthony, E.J. (1957) *Group Psychotherapy.* Harmondsworth: Penguin.

Garland, J.A., Jones, H.E. and Kolodny, R.L. (1965) A Model for Stages of Development in Social Work Groups. In S. Bernstein (ed.) *Explorations in Groupwork.* Boston Univ. School of Social Work.

Hartford, M.E. (1972) *Groups in Social Work.* Boulder, Col.: Col. Univ. Press.

McCullough, M.K. and Ely, P.J. (1969) *Social Work with Groups.* London: Routledge and Kegan Paul.

McLennan, B.W. and Felsenfeld, N. (1968) *Group Counselling and Psychotherapy with Adolescents.* Boulder, Col.: Col. Univ. Press.

Northen, H. (1969) *Social Work with Groups.* Boulder, Col.: Col. Univ. Press.

Richardson, E. (1967) *Group Study for Teachers.* London: Routledge and Kegan Paul.

Schutz, W.C. (1958). *F.I.R.O. A Three-dimensional Theory of Interpersonal Orientations.* N.Y.: Holt, Rinehart and Winston.

Solomon, B.B. (1968). Social Group Work in the Adult Outpatient Clinic. *Social Work* (US).

Walton, H. (ed.) (1971) *Small Group Psychotherapy.* Harmondsworth: Penguin.

Glossary

Affective Ties — Bonds of liking (affection) between members of a group. They may be in existence from the beginning of a natural group (friendship group), or may be the result of shared experience in a convened group and are an essential feature of the development of trust and consequently of the group's ability to work effectively together.

Aggregate — The first convening of any collection of people is an aggregate until they interact and begin to take on meaningful relationships and establish some form. A gathering of people without a common bond or significant interaction.

Attraction To A Group — The main reason why people stay in any group of which they are a member. Thus as long as a member obtains satisfactions from his membership greater than any that he can expect from changing his membership he will remain in the group. The greater a member's attraction to a given group the more control the group will have over his behaviour. (See *Cohesion.*)

Authentic Interaction — This occurs when persistent incongruous behaviour by a member of a group is persistently reflected back to him by other members, creating in the member a psychological crisis because he is forced to re-evaluate his self-image. As long as the other members are seen as caring the first member's behaviour will tend to change and become more congruent:

> 'The sequence repeats itself at one time or another involving all members. Each time the sequence recurs it involves more people who are becoming more congruent and, hence, tends to improve. As people are thus helped more, deeper feelings are experienced and the amount of time spent in the present increases. The longer the group lasts, the more helpfully and authentically do members interact.' (Golombiewski and Blumberg, 1970: 118)

Interaction which produces self-understanding and congruent behaviour.

Autonomous Groups — gangs, street clubs, cliques, families. Groups which are formed spontaneously by the people who become members of the group — otherwise referred to as 'natural' groups, 'self-formed' — or 'member-formed' groups. Self-governing — without outside control.

Bond — Another term for group attraction and group cohesion. It identifies the mass of ties which unite the members of a group. Thus if the group bond is strong members identify with the group, obtain high satisfaction levels from their membership and are subject to high levels of influence in their individual behaviour by group standards. Bond is not equal for all members of a group as peripheral members may be less satisfied with their position.

Brain Storming — A technique of spontaneous reaction to ideas. Usually performed by a group in order to put forward as many ideas as possible in a short time about a given area in order to produce some basis for consideration. Large sheets of paper or blackboards are placed before the group, the area for consideration easily visible, members are asked to shout out any idea which comes to mind no matter how apparently irrelevant. The statements are recorded and provide a visual stimulus to associated ideas as well as the verbal stimuli. The mass of material thus recorded usually shows many associations of ideas which have been pulled out which would not have been available if deliberately conscious thought processes had been followed.

Buzz Techniques — A method of getting interaction in a large formally arranged group by requesting people to turn round to face those behind them and form small groups. Material which has just been presented to the group can then be discussed by these small groupings and the result of the discussion fed back for the benefit of the total group after some minutes.

Change Agent — Originally the person who dealt with the 'transfer' problem in T. Groups, i.e. the problem of transferring a group started on the basis of members being strangers to one in which members had familial relationships or vice versa. More recently the group operator who diagnoses and prescribes, usually in the context of an organization.

Thus the change agent is any person who 'is preoccupied with the transfer problem, with searching for ways and means to apply the accumulating results of the behavioural sciences in a wide variety of contexts'. A person who attempts beneficial modifications (W.G. Bennis 'The Change Agents'. In Golembiewski and Blumberg, 1970: 306-10).

Check List — Usually refers to either (i) a sequence of factors which need to be checked before a group is established in order to place the group on a firm foundation, or (ii) an evaluation of various points of a group's behaviour in order to establish its movement, direction, and nature.

Climate — Generally speaking the atmosphere of a group, which is engendered by the emotional factors operating within a group. When this psychological or emotional atmosphere is fairly constant this then constitutes the climate of the group, e.g. anxiety, confidence etc. Probably there are two main climates, those which are defensive in nature and those which are supportive.

Closed Group — A group which is convened with a given number of members and to which no new members are admitted during the life of the group. Some authorities maintain that no group is totally closed in the sense that most members of a given group bring into, and take away from the group, experiences. Thus every group's boundaries are demarcation points in ongoing life experience rather than walls encapsulating a total isolate existence.

Cohesion — Some groups gel, others do not. Many factors seem to be responsible for a group following either course. Chief amongst those which appear to enhance cohesion in a group are such things as a high level of attraction to the group for individual members, a general sense of acceptance and belonging, and the satisfaction of needs. Well-established groups tend to respond to an external threat by increasing their cohesion. This bond implies a united group with a level of trust which makes mutual support readily available and creates a strong identification for members with the group. (See *Bond*.)

Co-Leader — Works in conjunction with the leader — usually in the role of observer/analyser. He may take on the role of socio-emotional leader complementing the task orientation of the leader. In marital counselling in groups co-leadership offers a role model for group members of two people operating in harmonious efficiency.
One important job may be to observe the leader and report on blind spots in order to enhance his performance.

Collusion — Agreement in group decision-making is frequently achieved by tacit acceptance on the part of group members rather than by explicit expressed agreement. If decisions made in this way are questioned later group members are faced with the fact that lack of positive expressed disagreement has been taken as acceptance. Many forms of collusion occur in group life and a part of the task of sensitizing members to their own and others' behaviour is to enhance recognition of behaviour which is collusive so that members may have a more conscious control over their part in the group's existence.

Conflict — 'At the group level, conflict may lead to enhanced understanding and consequent strengthening of relationships among members because differences are aired and not allowed to remain irritatingly below the surface — provides stimulation and a basis for interaction.'

'Realistic conflict is tied to a rational goal and the conflict concerns the means of achieving the goal. In unrealistic conflict the conflict becomes the end itself.' (Northen, 1969: 42)

Confrontation — '. . . attempts to encourage group participants to join in a mutual escalation of truthfulness, so as to reverse

degenerative feedback sequences. It has a compelling internal
logic which encourages owning and openness concerning
organisational issues, with the goals of increasing mutual trust
and decreasing the perceived risk of owning and being open.'
(Golembiewski and Blumberg 1970: 385)

Consensus — Group democracy allows of decisions based on the
wishes of the majority. Consensus is thus the assent of the larger
number of members to a given proposition. Tacit assent may
contain elements of collusion and in order to ensure (a) that
consensus exists and (b) that its apparent existence is not the
result of lack of understanding, apathy, or lack of clarity about
the issues involved, testing can take place.
Consensus testing usually takes the form of a direct request to
the group members either individually or as a group whether they
agree or disagree with the proposition under consideration.

Content — What a group is talking about. Content of a conversation is the subject-matter.

Contract — 'Goals can become a group product only as they are
discussed, considered, and made fairly explicit by the group
members together through some deliberative process . . . this
process by which the group comes to some conclusion about the
nature of its business and direction is referred to as "setting a
contract".' (Hartford, 1972: 142)

Hence contract groups are those in which the goals are clearly
outlined before the group is convened and agreed to by the
parties concerned. The contract is explicit. Each method of
forming a group usually contains within it an implicit contract
which needs to be understood and usually made explicit. (See
Part 2, chapter 3)

Decision-Making — A process in individuals or groups concerned
with arriving at some solution of perceived problems. The process
usually follows the sequence:
1) identification of the problem
2) proposals for solution
3) analysis of the proposals
4) the actual choice or decision.
Many other factors are possibly involved, e.g. outside resources,
clarification procedures, the emotions, beliefs, and experience of

the members involved. Many decisions are made in groups with no clear appreciation of how they were arrived at. It is part of the group trainer's task to ensure that members become aware of the processes involved.

Defence Mechanisms — There are a number of mechanisms which are frequently used to protect the self, that is, to help in maintaining self-esteem. Some of these are:

1	rationalization	— a good reason, but not the real reason.
2	projection	— ascribing one's own secret wishes, shortcomings, etc., to another.
3	repression	— forgetting or ignoring the unpleasant.
4	regression	— reverting to a more primitive form of behaviour to get what one wants.
5	reaction-formation	— repressing feeling of guilt and acting in the opposite way.
6	withdrawal	— day-dreaming, fantasies.
7	insulation	— failure to see incompatible ideas; establishing 'logic-tight' compartments.
8	sublimation	— converting an anti-social desire into an acceptable channel.
9	displacement	— rechannelling energy from a blocked goal to an unblocked goal.

Development — Groups are likened to organisms possessing a growth potential. Thus any group tends to have a life-span and to go through stages of development. Usually this is not only sequential but tends to be cumulative, that is, progression is not regular but contains regressive interludes. Generally, if a group continues to exist, it develops to the point where its task is completed or as near to this state as is possible and then declines and comes to an end. Some things which are easily achieved by a group in one stage of development are hard or impossible in another. It is an essential requisite of groupwork practice to be able to recognize at least the general stage of development of a group.

Duration — Used of the length of time a particular group is in existence, not of the length of a particular session within a group's life.

Dyads — The smallest possible group comprises two persons. In order to eliminate many of the complexities of relationships in larger groups experimenters frequently used dyads to establish basic group behaviours. It is sometimes maintained that all large groups are composed of dyads and triads (threes) in constant and changing relationships to each other according to purpose.

Encounter – (a) the original meeting of strangers in a newly formed group.

(b) in Rogerian theory, 'the quality of the inter-personal encounter with the client which is the most significant element in determinining effectiveness'. This quality is compounded of factors like congruence, empathy, positive regard and unconditionality of regard, all of which need to be perceived by the client, i.e. communicated to him, to be effective.

Expectations – Any new member of a group brings with him his own norms based on past experience. He has no 'experimental base' for knowing what to expect of the group, or what the group expects of him. Wide disparities of expectations frustrate members in their use of the group, and group workers need to develop 'mutuality of expectations' between themselves and the group. Expectations are thus said to be 'cleared' and a commonly accepted basis for working is arrived at.

Experiential Learning – Learning by experience – a favourite method of instructing people about group processes by using the actual group of learners as a model of group behaviour. Commonly called by group trainers 'Gut learning' it is concerned with expanding conscious experience in structured and controlled situations.

Feedback – In everyday life assumptions are made by people about the reasons for the observed behaviour of others – and actions and attitudes are usually based on these assumptions. Feedback is a technique of ascertaining what people know or feel about their behaviour and attitudes which can then be compared with assumptions about it and some more realistic or authentic understanding achieved.

Feedback is also used to describe a technique of eliciting response from groups or individuals about work or thinking they have performed in a large group situation so that it becomes available to all.

Fight — One method of coping with unfinished business (*vide*) by engaging the other group member involved in conflict. In Bion's terminology the whole group may indulge in this kind of behaviour — a temporary strategy which may be necessary but eventually needs resolution.

Flight — Another method of coping with unfinished business (*vide*) is by avoiding the issue. Again in Bion's words the whole group may evade the issue of the group's task. Evasion may be effected by substitution of some inoffensive matter — a temporary but sometimes necessary solution.

Followership — A necessary and complementary concept to that of leadership. No one can lead in a group situation unless others are prepared to follow. A tacit acceptance of leadership by members contains the implicit assumption that they have no wish at that moment in time to oppose the leader or challenge him for his position. Followers may have a less responsible role in some ways than leaders, but full recognition of their democratic equality and right to disagree and challenge should be observed.

Followership has important implications for designated leaders — (imposed leadership).

Group Influences — 'When an individual is in a social situation he tends to react toward himself in the same way that he thinks others would react to him' (Mead 1934). Thus a group can exert considerable influence on an individual's behaviour, especially in so far as the member has a strong attachment to the group and other members, to the group norms and values, to his status in the group, and the rewards and sanctions available to enforce conformity. The more the group meets an individual's needs the greater the group's influence on that member, given there is no readily available substitute.

Group Therapy — The treatment of people in groups. It may be individual-centred, i.e. treating one person in a group, or group-centred, i.e. treating the group as a unit. Treatment is usually based upon the facts that groups provide:
a) a realistic life situation
b) many common problems
c) a bond between members and a desire to help each other
d) a controlled familial experience

e) mutual acceptance, affection, respect, and helpfulness.
The main schools of group therapy are:

Psychoanalytic	Moreno (sociometry)
Adlerian	General semantics approach
Rogerian	Gestalt.

Helping Relationship — Is given different names, e.g. counselling, teaching, guiding, training, educating, etc. They have in common that the helping person is trying to influence (and therefore change) the individual who is being helped, and that the direction of the change will be constructive and useful to him (i.e. clarify his perceptions of the problem, bolster his self-confidence, modify his behaviour, or develop new skills, etc.).

Figure 10

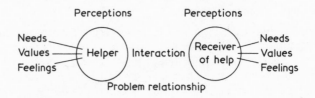

Here and Now — Implies that the basic focus of the group is on what is happening at the moment — it is the current behaviour that is immediately relevant to the learning experience of the group, not what has transpired previously.

Hidden Agenda —

'Although total group goals are generally avowed, expressed,

and understood by all members, the "secret" expectations held
by individual members, organizers, or subgroups may influence
the direction of group goals. These have been labelled 'hidden
agenda' and may distort or redirect the planning or action of
the group . . . hidden agendas are not necessarily malicious or
even conscious attempts to disrupt the group's process . . .
members are not even aware that they are acting on a hidden
agenda.' (Hartford, 1972: 141-2)

I.P.A. – *Interaction Process Analysis* a recording scale developed
by R.F. Bales (1950) which allows group interaction to be rated
quickly not only in terms of who talked but also of the type of
contribution. (The full scale appears in Part 2, chapter 6).

Interaction – The group is viewed as a system of patterns and
sequences of communicative acts by members. Interaction is
therefore 'the dynamic interplay of forces in which contract
between persons results in a modification of the attitudes and
behaviour of the participants.' Communication, both verbal and
non-verbal, is basic to interaction.

Intake Process – The procedure by which members are
approached by the group worker and prepared for admission to
the group. The main considerations being that of clearing
objectives, assessing suitability, and forming links between
members.

Interpretation – A technique of clarification based upon
theoretical understanding of human behaviour, the object of
which is to enhance members' understanding of what is going on
and to increase their choice of behaviour and their conscious
control.

Intervention– Conscious interference in group processes in order
to move the group towards its goal or to introduce clarification,
enlightenment, or a change in direction. It is in all aspects an
exercise of control and of power.

Isolates –
    'The social isolate is the person who is present but generally
    ignored by the others. He does not seem to reach out to
    others, or he reaches out but is rejected. His lack of affiliation
    with others in the group may be due to lack of capacity on
    his part to get along with others, or he may differ in values,

beliefs, and life style from the others enough to be a deviant. He is not generally the scapegoat, for if he were he would be getting attention, however negative.

The true isolate is ignored, his contributions go unnoticed, his opinions are not asked for.' (Hartford, 1972: 208)

Laboratory Approach – Stems from an inter-group relations workshop held at Connecticut in 1946, which developed into the National Training Laboratory for Group Development (NTL) at Bethel, Maine, in 1947. Its main tool is the T. Group, described as follows:

(1)   It is an experience in creating a miniature society
(2)   It is oriented toward working with processes that emphasize inquiry, exploration and experimentation with behaviour.
(3)   It is oriented toward helping members to learn.
(4)   It is oriented toward developing a psychologically safe atmosphere that facilitates learning.
(5)   What is to be learned is largely determined by its members, although a professional 'trainer' is usually available to provide guidance.

(Golembiewski and Blumberg, 1970: 5-6)

Length of Session – There is little research in this area of practice. Hartford says 'length of session is largely a matter of preference and capacity of members.' It may depend on the time available, the stage of development of the group, the kind of task in hand, the concentration span of the members, etc. Marathon groups lasting several days have been used 'to operate on the fatigue factor and the contagion factor of breaking down defences . . . ' (Hartford, 1972: 187).

Maintenance – The function of maintaining the group, i.e. attempting to keep the group in good working order, to create a harmonious working atmosphere and to enhance good relationships.

These are otherwise known as the socioemotional functions and form the major task of any co-leader to complement the leader's task-oriented or instrumental behaviour. Obviously energy spent on relationship problems is energy diverted from the group task. The function ensuring the minimum need for such energy application is a necessary one in order to enhance group performance.

Membership — The individuals who make up a group — who are aware of belonging to the group, who gain satisfaction of some needs by being part of the group. Processes of selection are usually employed to determine an individual's suitability for membership of a given group. Factors involved may include social background, age, sex, ethnic, and sociometric status, personality variables, problem orientation, availability, etc.

Natural Group — Self-governing groups — which arise spontaneously from ordinary circumstances (*See Autonomous Groups.*)

Newcomer — Phenomenon of open groups in which members can come in or leave during the life of the group. The problem of the introduction of a new member to an established group highlights the essential nature of shared experience in the establishment of group relationships. Any newcomer may have had similar experience to the members of the group he is joining but it has not been shared with them. Most open groups establish some kind of formal or informal ritual procedure for the vetting and introduction of newcomers. The informal procedure may be expedited by a period of preparation both of the group and the newcomer.

The advent of a newcomer illuminates briefly most of the dynamics of the group situation.

Non-Directive Techniques — In group and individual counselling non-directive techniques consist of methods of helping people to express their thoughts, beliefs, attitudes and feelings by responding at the level at which material is offered. This implies that even if the counsellor or group leader is aware that the information being disclosed would indicate movement in any given direction he does not either tell the counsellee of his interpretation or endeavour to guide him in this direction. The counsellee must use the counsellor to clarify and reflect his own ideas and through this come to a more realistic understanding of his problems and difficulties.

Non-Verbal Communication — The most commonly accepted method of communication is verbal — hence the enormous emphasis on the value of words, speech, writing and definitions. However, human beings also communicate by other kinds of symbols e.g. gesture, postures, ritualized behaviour, etc. Significantly these symbolic communications have great value in view of the common acceptance that words are as frequently used to evade or obscure as they are to clarify. When the communication cues which are offered are disparate i.e. between speech and behaviour, then the latter is much more likely to be accepted as conveying the true state of affairs, particularly when the concern of the communication is with emotions and feelings rather than facts. Exercises can be developed which enhance understanding of non-verbal communication and interpretation of it. Many communication cues are not consciously controlled and it is for this reason that greater reliance is placed upon the truth of the non-verbal cues.

Norms – The patterns of acceptable behaviour which any group establishes over a period of time. Levels of conformity with these patterns are established and rewards given for compliance, sanctions applied for nonconformity. They constitute the rules of behaviour explicit or implicit of any group and need to be mastered by any newcomer before he can be totally accepted.

Observing – The observation of performance, of the personality in action, based on the assumption that people are what they do. The techniques of observing and recording group behaviour are discussed in Part 2 Chapter 6.

Open-ended Group – Groups in which the membership changes during the total existence of the group. Members may leave or newcomers arrive; as long as the central core of the group possesses sufficient stability to allow on-going shared experience for its members, the group can exist as a unit.

Organizational Development Groups

'evolved in the early 1960s: as a modification of the basic T. Group. Their rationale was that our day-to-day behaviour is the product of the pressures due to our roles in the organisations in which we work. If training is to be relevant to performance within a particular organisation, then it needs to be done within that organisation. Development of the organisation as a team is the goal rather than of the individual as a person. If one assembled for discussion of here-and-now behaviour an entire work group consisting of an industrial manager and his various subordinates, or a school headmaster and his department heads, the result would be an organisational development group . . . The leader of the group is likely to be the senior man present rather than the external consultant or trainer. The external consultant's role will depend on the needs of the group, but it most likely covers questions and comments about existing procedures.'

(P.B. Smith, 1971)

Pairing – A supportive technique by two group members which involves a collusive agreement of each to back up the moves of the other. It is one method by which a group member who is not too confident of his ability to put forward his point of view, either verbally or otherwise, or is not certain of the reception he may get when he does, looks for and gets support from another member whom he suspects of maintaining a sympathetic viewpoint.

It can be useful in bringing out otherwise hidden ideas, but it can also be used to defeat the growing purpose of the group. It is a temporary subgroup formation or an alliance. (See *Unfinished Business.*)

Personal Growth – When sensitivity training is used with a basic philosophy that man is alienated, has problems of identity and autonomy, lacks understanding of his own internal environment and the ability to communicate with others – then 'personal' growth' is the goal of the training. These groups are an attempt to 'open people up, to free them from inhibitions, and to get them to express their pent-up feelings.' (P.B. Smith, 25 March 1971, 'Varieties of Group Experience', *New Society*). (See *Encounter.*)

Planned Organizational Change – The overall effect achieved by a successful organizational development exercise in which the changes are planned, based upon the learning processes which have taken place within the group.

Power – Power may be defined as the ability to influence the behaviour of others consciously and deliberately. French and Raven (1959) indicate that there are five bases of social power: 1) the power of reward

2) the power to punish or coerce
3) legitimate power
4) specialist power
5) referent power

In all cases power tends to be awarded by others because they see or believe that the person in question (or group) possesses certain abilities. A rule of thumb about power says that whenever one person possesses something which another person wishes to have, the first person also may be seen to have power over the second. Obviously the ability to reward and punish are the simplest ways in which power to influence may be seen by others. Legitimate power is that which is delegated to a person or group by a higher, greater acknowledged authority. Historically, kings were legitimized by being appointed traditionally under the authority of God (Divine Right). Specialist power derives from the recognition that the specialist possesses knowledge, skill, and expertise valuable to the group in the achievement of their tasks and goals. Finally referent power is seen as being possessed by the person who has those qualities admired and emulated by others.

An analysis of the power structure of any group yields valuable information for the members, and awareness of the way each member exercises power and yields to its exercise in others is part of the growing understanding of the nature of authentic interaction in a developing group.

Problem-solving – '. . . the creative process by which individuals (and groups) evaluate changes in themselves and their environment, and make new choices, decisions or adjustments in harmony with life goals and values, which may also be in a state of flux. Thus conceived, problem-solving is a fundamental technique of living in a democratic social order.' (M.E. Bennett, 1963: 114).

'The problem-solving process has certain sequential phases that follow each other in a fairly regular way, each phase being dependent upon the preceding one and each influencing those that follow.' (H. Northen, 1969: 16). (See also *Decision-Making*.)

Process – The way in which a group handles its communication, i.e. who talks? how much? or who talks to whom?

Psychodrama – Moreno, elaborating on the cathartic effects of Greek tragedy and of custom, folklore, and ritual drama, developed the concept of psychodrama. There are many techniques but the basic idea remains constant in all. That is that drama allows expression of feelings and attitudes which have long been suppressed and hidden and that such expression frees the patient from the pressures of maintaining his lack of conscious awareness of their influence.

Psychodrama is used mainly for disturbed patients in a hospital or clinic setting. In its commonest form a patient selects a significant period in his life and casts other patients in the roles of the others involved with him. Sufficient information is given about these roles for the patients to play them effectively, frequently drawing largely on their own experience in a similar role. The drama is then played out before an audience who join in critical discussion at the end. Role changes and reversals can be used to highlight certain interactions. The main function of the drama is to spotlight for the patient a projected image of his behaviour outside himself so that he can look at it and hopefully learn about himself in the process. (See also *Sociodrama*.)

Purpose – 'Purpose dictates practice.' The essential reason for the existence of a group is its purpose; all other factors are initially and continually influenced by this basic fact. Purpose provides the framework within which all other group activities may be seen to be related.

Rating Methods – Several methods of assessing a group's progress exist (see *I.P.A.*). The simplest is to ask members to fill in a questionnaire which asks them to rate statements about the group. Overall perceptions of movement and individual variations may then be revealed. (Examples can be studied in Part 2 Chapter 6.)

Reaching Out – (1) The group worker's need to recognize the full extent of his position and strength in the group situation and to use these assets to move toward group members and to help them to exercise their membership roles more effectively.
(2) Northen uses this term of social workers seeking out people thought to be in need who have not themselves sought social work help. Group discussions are frequently used to indicate to such people the kind of service which is available to them.

Reaction to Threat – Individuals respond to what they perceive as a threat to their esteem and security in ways learned through previous experience; they cover the whole gamut of defensive reactions from anger to withdrawal.

Recorder — A member of the group with the special responsibility of recording in some tangible form the activities and decisions of the group. The role tends to be isolated from that of leader because the act of recording effectively requires considerable application and concentration which would handicap a leader in the full performance of his role.

Resource Person — Any person in or out of a group who is regarded by the group as possessing specialist skills, knowledge, or abilities which would assist the group in the achievement of its goal or goals.

Scapegoating — The name stems directly from the Bible — the goat symbolically loaded with the sins of the community and driven out into the wilderness. Hence the current use applies to group members who are selected or select themselves to be the recipient of the bad feelings which other group members cannot face in themselves. The scapegoat burdened in this way becomes an object of some derision and the others feel relieved of their bad feelings. Scapegoats are seldom truly driven out because they are far too useful.

Another form of scapegoating occurs when a group is preparing to take a move forward and one member hangs back in uncertainty — this member then receives all the scorn that partially resolved anxiety on the part of the other members can muster. This usually frees the group to move as planned — the scapegoat performs a very useful maintenance function.

Sensitivity Training — Experience-based learning — members work together in small groups over a period of time, learning through analysis of their own experiences, feelings, reactions, perceptions, and behaviour. Each member is responsible for his own learning. The trainer's role is to facilitate the examination and understanding of experiences within the group. Members are encouraged to conceptualize about their group experience. A person is free to learn when he establishes *authentic relationships* with other people, increasing his self-esteem and decreasing his defences. Members acquire new skills in working with people and examine the value system on which they are based. (See also *T. Groups and Laboratory Approach*.)

Silence – 'The art of creative listening lies in the ability to remain receptively silent.' (S.R. Slavson, 1961)

Silence in a group can indicate:

(i) disinterest

(ii) the leader's attempt to enhance the group's self-direction

(iii) support and confidence

(iv) shared feelings

(v) reflection

(vi) resistance

Silence can be threatening and needs careful analysis by the group leader before appropriate action is taken.

Size – A very sensitive factor in any group. Most group work situations involve small groups i.e. five to fifteen members. Where maximum interaction is needed in a group then the smaller sizes are more effective simply, but not solely, because of the increased possibility (a) of contact and (b) of participation. (See chapter 5.)

Sociodrama – A form of role-play in which a prepared drama is staged, based on a particular social problem. Two basic effects are involved (i) therapeutic, where the problem is concerned with personal factors, e.g. relationships, and the learning which derives from the performance is instrumental in enhancing personal awareness and in increasing adaptive behaviour, and (ii) educational, where the problem is one concerned with possible solutions to social problems and the drama is used as 'try on' to see how each solution would appear in real life.

A frequent spin-off from any sociodrama is enhanced understanding by each participant of the resources at his command and also of the way other people may feel. (See also *Psychodrama*.)

Sociogram – A graphic method of depicting the choice-relationship formed by the use of a sociometric test. The most usual choices asked for are based on questions like 'With whom would you like to work?', or 'With whom would you like to sit?', always based upon an actual situation in which selection is a serious consideration and containing an element of freedom for the choosing members to be disposed according to their choice.

Sociograms may also be used as recording devices indicating not choices but factors like 'Who spoke to whom'. An example of this use may be found in Part 2 Chapter 6.

Stereotyping — When people are assessed upon minimal selected evidence stereotyping takes place. It is thus a form of selective blindness in that what is believed to be true of a given person or group tends to receive confirmation from the clues received by the believer and other clues which would offer evidence contradicting or modifying the belief are monitored out.

In group situations ample scope exists for stereotypes to be seen for the plastic images they are and for more of the actual person to be revealed.

Subgroups — 'As members of a group come to discover what they have in common, various subgroups develop which are expressive of common interests, mutuality of feelings, of attraction or repulsion, or needs for control and inclusion. The smallest subgroup is the pair or dyad . . . ' (Northen, 1969: 31).

Larger groups have a tendency to produce more subgroup formation. From subgroups may come challenge to the accepted direction of the group or they may be the centres of new ideas, forward movement, or specific interests.

Tasks — Usually task is held to be the same as the group purpose or goal, but it is also taken to mean some part of an overall goal in the sense that complete goals may be achieved by the performance of a series of tasks. Orientation toward the task is one of the main functions of leadership.

Termination — As a group is created and lives, it also dies. Termination is therefore a conscious aim both of the leader and the group either upon completion of the task or upon realization that its achievement is not feasible. Disintegration is an automatic process in an ailing group — termination is a process which allows withdrawal of commitment by the group members, disengagement usually in the reverse order in which commitment was built up, e.g. through affection into control, and finally inclusion.

There And Then — Otherwise known as the 'back home' situation, this term refers to the past in contrast to the current 'here and now' emphasis of much groupwork. The past is frequently used as an evasive technique.

Learning which takes place in the present has many applications in the 'back home' situation.

Threat — When members or groups perceive a person or situation which increases their anxiety and sense of inadequacy they are said to be experiencing threat. Its main manifestations are a sense of being exposed, undefended, attacked or overwhelmed. Responses cover the whole gamut of defences. (See *Reaction To Threat*.)

Time — Time is a factor which is frequently overlooked. Its effect upon the group's development and thus upon the way it works is of paramount importance, particularly in the compelling effect it may have on decision-making.

Training Groups — Training groups are otherwise known as sensitivity groups or T. groups. The members, usually strangers, meet in a setting away from outside distractions for periods of up to ten days. The leader encourages them to look at the way their behaviour is affecting one another on the basis that their effectiveness as individuals is intimately bound up with their relations to others. Members are encouraged to talk freely and openly about all aspects of their relationship with others.

Treatment — When a group is used to effect change in one or all of its members, where this change is based upon an assessment of the needs and potential of the group and is engineered for their benefit — then a treatment situation is in being. Continuous evaluation of the effects of treatment are essential in order that beneficial effects may be enhanced and harmful effects reduced.

Triads — Three persons form a triad. Some authorities maintain that this is the largest group in which intense relationships can exist. All larger groups are thus seen as composed of a fluctuating pattern of threes, twos, and ones — the pattern emerging because members relate more frequently to some members than others.

Unfinished Business (See Jo-Harri window, p.118)

'Consider the case in which A becomes aware of a feeling or thought about himself or others and does not disclose this information. This enlarges the "Hidden Area", and accumulates what is called "unfinished business". That business acts as an unresolved tension system that interferes with the individual's ability to operate effectively and congruently (see *Encounter*) in relation to others. By the same token, if A's behaviour hinders B — blocks him from behaving congruently with his feelings for example — B develops unfinished business with A and increases the "Blind Area" until he openly deals with A's unawareness.' (Golembiewski and Blumberg, 1970: 62)

Methods of coping with unfinished business are 'fight', 'flight', pairing and confronting.

Unfreeze — Group trainer's term implying a reduction in social-distance-maintaining behaviour. It implies a development of trust between members who consequently become less guarded, more honest and sincere. Interaction between them becomes authentic and the possibility of increasing self-awareness and sensitivity is greatly enhanced.

Ventilation — The cathartic expression of feelings. A freeing and cleansing process which frees individuals and groups from the emotional pressures of maintaining defensive attitudes in certain areas of experience. Ventilation implies a level of trust, e.g. that advantage will not be taken by others of the exposure. It also helps to clear the air in that assumptions about other members' behaviour, beliefs, and feelings can be compared with their expression of them and a more realistic appraisal and assessment made.

Withdrawal — Physical withdrawal means actually leaving a group. But psychological withdrawal takes several forms. Thus members may opt out of the group proceedings by paying attention to other things, becoming absorbed in their own thought processes, day-dreaming, sleeping, and also by positive actions which dissociate them from the group. Causes are many: boredom, anxiety, lack of understanding, overwhelming pressures from external sources, tiredness, illness, lack of sympathy, anger, frustration, etc.

REFERENCES

Bales, R.F. (1950) *Interaction Process Analysis: A Method for the Study of Small Groups.* Reading, Mass.: Addison-Wesley.
Bennett, M.E. (1963) *Guidance and Counselling in Groups.* NY: McGraw-Hill.
Bion, W.R. (1961) *Experience in Groups.* London: Tavistock.
French, J.R.P. and Raven, B. (1959) 'The Bases of Social Power.

In *Studies in Social Power.* Ann Arbor: Michigan Inst. for Soc. Research.

Golembiewski, R.T. and Blumberg, A. (1970) *Sensitivity Training and the Laboratory Approach.* Itasca, Ill.: F.E. Peacock

Hartford, M.E. (1972) *Groups in Social Work.* Boulder, Colorado: Col. Univ. Press.

Mead, G.H. (1934) *Mind, Self and Society.* Chicago: Univ. of Chicago Press.

Northen, H. (1969) *Social Work with Groups.* Boulder, Colorado: Col. Univ. Press.

Slavson, S.R. (1961) *Re-educating the Delinquent.* NY.: Collier Macmillan.

Smith, P.B. (March 1971) Varieties of Group Experience. *New Society.*

Annotated Reading List

This reading list is divided into five parts:

1) General texts on groupwork
2) Other texts containing usable material
3) Readers and collections of relevant articles
4) Selected British material on practice
5) Other relevant articles

(British texts are marked with an asterisk.)

1) General Texts

Margaret E. Bennett (1963) (revised ed.) *Guidance and Counselling in Groups.* NY: McGraw-Hill.

> A wide-ranging text on group counselling of only general interest to most social workers. However, chapters 4, 5 and 6 offer a fairly basic but quick guide to the theory of group dynamics and group psychotherapy.

*Tom Douglas (1970) *A Decade of Small Group Theory 1960-1970.* Bristol: Bookstall Publications.

> A short text covering the more essential theoretical material produced between 1960-70, and its applicability to groupwork practice. It covers (1) group composition (2) group development (3) the role of the group worker (4) intervention strategies (5) isolates, and other points.
>
> There is a good bibliography.

Margaret E. Hartford (1972) *Groups in Social Work.* NY: Columbia University Press.

> A good general text on groupwork well related to the available research, and focused on groups (a) designed to enhance personal functioning, and (b) to effect social change. The chapters are — (1) Groups in social work (2) Social science findings in the use of groups (3) Phases in group development (4) Group composition and membership (5) Group goals (6) Size, space and time (7) Interaction process and inter-

personal relationships (8) Deliberation and decision-making in the group (9) Cohesion (10) Group influence and control and the evolution of group culture.

There is an extensive American bibliography.

Alan F. Klein (1970) *Social Work through Group Process.* State University of Albany: School of Social Welfare.

This is a personal and eclectic approach to groupwork which sets out to present the author's belief about the knowledge and assumptions which lie behind the use of groups in social work. It is well worth reading for this material alone which comprises chapters 1 and 2. Section 11 (chapters 3, 4, 5 and 6) presents the author's model of group methods, and the remaining sections contain some comment on practice in various settings and a critique of small group theory and social research.

Sometimes confusing and confused this text offers a welcome respite from the theorists who believe that groups are either treatment-oriented and social action-oriented or task-oriented, etc. Klein believes that the approach should be suited to the job in hand and may combine many elements or only one and that the combination can and should change as circumstances change.

Gisela Konopka (1963) *Social Groupwork: a Helping Process.* Englewood Cliffs, N.J.: Prentice-Hall.

A good general text which never seems to get to the meat and has now been superseded by texts which rely more upon research findings and less upon descriptive material. Konopka is however very readable and is concerned a great deal with the ethics of the situations she writes about.

There is an interesting but dated bibliography.

*M.K. McCullough and Peter J. Ely (1968) *Social Work with Groups.* (Library of Social Work) London: Routledge and Kegan Paul.

A very practical little book in the mechanics of setting up and running a group, based upon practical experience. The theoretical orientation is almost exclusively psychoanalytic and in this sense it is a product of its time and needs to be seen in the context of the massive increase of recent years in material from other sources relevant to group practice.

*Fred Milson (1973) *An Introduction to Groupwork Skill.* London: Routledge and Kegan Paul.

This is not really a text for social work group workers, but is directed at the peripheral areas of social work. There is good material about observation in groups which is valuable in so far as little enough is written about this basic skill. There are few clearly expressed theoretical orientations which would allow a reader to understand Milson's approach.

Rodney W. Napier and Matti K. Gershenfeld (1973) *Groups: Theory and Experience.* Boston: Houghton Mifflen.

This text is not aimed specifically at professional social workers but at what the authors refer to as 'facilitators'. Its emphasis is decidedly in the area of the enhancement of personal growth and offers exercises which are designed to secure experiential as well as intellectual learning. There is emphasis on research material and good chapters are: 1) Perception and communication; 5) Leadership; 7) The evolution of working groups: understanding and prediction. Several of the games and exercises are also very well worthwhile e.g. The three stage rocket; Communication role reversal, etc.

Helen Northen (1969) *Social Work with Groups*. NY: Columbia University Press.

Apart from the introductory chapters the book is designed to cover the developmental sequence of a group. Thus it starts with planning and setting up and ends with termination, each part dealing with the peculiar problems of group life at different stages of development. Basically this text is concerned with treatment-oriented groups and contains a wealth of information which is however not clearly related to any expressed theoretical orientation. There is an excellent American bibliography and the book is eminently readable.

Sheila Thompson and J.H. Kahn (1970) *The Group Process as a Helping Technique.* Oxford: Pergamon Press.

This book is mainly concerned with:
a) group psychotherapy
b) group counsellings
c) group discussion
In the course of discussion of these three 'systems', some large

areas of theory related to groups are covered very lightly.
Examples are given of each of the 'systems' in operation.
However social group workers will tend to find that the
element of practical information is small and that the emphasis
on the leader-directed group almost excludes any understanding of self-directed groups.

2) Other Texts

*Michael Argyle (1970) *Social Interaction.* London: Methuen.
    An interesting book in the field of social psychology. There is
    a very interesting (for groupworkers) piece on 'five kinds of
    small social group' (1970: 240-266) concerned with the
    family; adolescent friendship groups; work groups; committees,
    problem-solving and creative groups; and finally T. groups and
    therapy groups.

*S.H. Foulkes and E.J. Anthony (1957) *Group Psychotherapy:
 The Psychoanalytic Approach.* Harmondsworth: Penguin.
    Published seventeen years ago this is still one of the most
    readable and informative texts on the psychoanalytic approach.
    is full of fascinating practical insights of great value to all
    group workers whatever their theoretical bias may be.

*Sue Jennings (1973) *Remedial Drama.* London: Pitman.
    This is not strictly a text about groupwork, but it is included
    here as a reminder that groups do not necessarily have to be
    founded on the basis of discussion. A delightfully simple book
    which looks at the use of drama in different settings and
    should give rise to ideas about the use of activity-based groups
    in many more situations than occur at present.

Matthew B. Miles (1971) *Learning to Work in Groups.* N.Y.:
Teachers College Press, Columbia University.
    Designed primarily for education circles, this is an essentially
    practical book about how to run groups of all kinds. It is
    especially good on the business of creating role-play situations
    as experiential learning. It contains a mass of games and
    exercises, many of which are practically useful as are the
    diagrams and recording ideas.

Nina Toren (1972) *Social Work: The Case of a Semi-Profession.*
Beverly Hills, Calif.: Sage Publications.

Part III of this book is devoted to 'Influence and change
through social group work'. Chapter 6 is concerned with the
purpose of groupwork, with techniques and some of the
theoretical background; Chapter 7 discusses the process of
influence in small groups and draws comparisons between the
'consequences of casework and groupwork', largely in favour
of the latter. Quite a lot of very useful and interesting material
is covered here very succinctly, with good references to
relevant research.

3) Readers

This kind of collected material seems to be on the increase both
in numbers and size, some volumes containing up to forty
contributions. In each book cited here only the more relevant
contributions will be noted.

Saul Bernstein (ed.) (1965) *Explorations in Group Work.* Boston:
Boston University School of Social Work.

There are four contributions in this collection, as follows:
1. 'Exploration and Working Agreement in Two Social Work
   Methods' – Louise Frey and Marguerite Meyer
2. 'A Model for Stages of Development in Social Work
   Groups' – James A. Garland, Hubert E. Jones and Ralph L.
   Kolodny
3. 'Conflict and Group Work' – Saul Bernstein
4. 'Decision-making and Group Work' – Louis Lowy

By far the most important contribution is the second which
offers an elaborate model of the stages of group development,
a concept which is essential to the understanding of the use of
treatment groups.

Saul Bernstein (ed.) (1970) *Further Explorations in Group Work,*
Boston: Boston University School of Social Work.

This contains seven contributions in which the stages of
development thesis is expanded and clarified and two other
articles are of value.
1. 'Application of Stages of Group Development to Groups in
   Psychiatric Settings' – James A. Garland and Louise A.
   Frey

demonstrates quite clearly the link between group development and a treatment plan, the influence of setting and the kind of people who are members of the group.
2. 'Group Composition as a Treatment Tool with Children' — Robert Paradise and Robert Daniels
   stresses the effect of selection and how this can be used positively as part of the treatment of the children within a group.
3. 'Characteristics and Resolution of Scapegoating' — James A. Garland and Ralph L. Kolodny
   This is a milestone of descriptive analysis. Despite the widely recognized and accepted fact of scapegoating there has been surprisingly little work done on it except in the area of prejudice. This article is essential reading for anyone who proposes to run groups.

Both these *Explorations* collections are highly committed to the concept of treatment in social work groups and it is advisable to remember this when attempting to translate any of this material into action.

Leland Bradford, Jack R. Gibb and Kenneth D. Benne (1964)
T. Group Theory and Laboratory Method. N.Y.: John Wiley.
   There are eighteen contributions here, and while there are simpler and more direct statements about T. groups, here will be found most of the information that the well-informed group practitioner needs to know about this particular area of group work. The editors draw upon other household names to augment their knowledge.

Dorwin Cartwright and Alvin Zander (1953) *Group Dynamics: Research and Theory.* London: Tavistock Publications.
   This book is still the basic text on group dynamics. For social workers, the commentary by the authors which precedes each group of contributions is perhaps more rewarding than the articles themselves.
   Particularly rewarding for social workers may well be:
   (3) 'Groups and Group Membership: Introduction' — Carter and Zander
   (7) 'The Nature of Group Cohesiveness' — Cartwright
   (20) 'The Bases of Social Power' — French and Raven
   (28) 'Personality and Situational Determinants of Leadership Effectiveness' — Fiedler

(30) 'Phases in Group Problem-Solving' — Bales and Strodtbeck

Perhaps the most effective studies are those about social power which can throw considerable light upon the social worker/client relationship, particularly in view of French and Raven's thesis that people are perceived by others as possessing power irrespective of whether the so-called 'possessor' of power is aware of how he is seen.

However this is a powerful book which will long continue to provide material for social workers.

Richard C. Diedrich and H. Allan Dye (1972) 'Group Procedures: Purposes, Processes and Outcomes'. In *Selected Readings for the Counsellor.* Boston: Houghton Mifflin.

This mammoth paperback contains forty contributions with many written by internationally known authors. It has one very large merit. Part Five which contains no less than seven articles presents the ethical problems of the use of groups in therapeutic settings and sensitivity training. All too often methods are presented without considerations of such problems.

The following contributions may be recommended:

6. 'What is Sensitivity Training?' — Charles Seashore
8. 'A Description of a Groupcentred Leader' — Thomas Gordon
10. 'An Inventory of Trainer Interventions' — William G. Dyer
16. 'The Process of the Basic Encounter Group' — Carl R. Rogers
19. 'Developmental Sequence in Small Groups' — Bruce W. Tuckman

*Joen Fagan and Irma Lee Shepherd (1972) *Gestalt Therapy Now: Theory, Techniques, Applications.* Harmondsworth: Penguin.

A fascinating reader for anyone interested in the development primarily by Frederick S. Perls of a therapy from Gestalt psychology. All of the book is very readable but the statements by Perls himself are rewarding. Many social workers may feel that this is the area of psychotherapy, but there is much that is applicable to social work groups especially when oriented toward personal growth.

Paul Glasser, Rosemary Sarri and Robert Vinter (1974) *Individual Change through Small Groups.* N.Y.: The Free Press.

This is a definitive statement by the University of Michigan School of Social Work. The group has produced thirty articles which cover most of the main ideas which the school has been putting forward about groupwork since the late 1950's. It is very difficult to select articles for mention here when most are worthwhile reading if only to get the idea of the logical thought which lies behind effective groupwork. Michigan are concerned to state the case for the treatment model of social group work and to this end tend to understate other approaches.

10. 'The Therapeutic Contract in Social Treatment' – Tom Croxton

16. 'A Comparison of Two Models of Social Group Work: The Treatment Model and the Reciprocal Model' – Sallie A. Churchill

11. 'Elements and Issues in Group Composition' – Harvey J. Bertcher and Frank Maple

have proved to be valuable and interesting. But the whole of Part I *A Conception of Practice* and Part II *The Treatment Sequence* should be read by all practitioners who want firm information about producing a treatment-oriented group.

Part IV is devoted to selected fields of practice and while interesting is the kind of material that may be found readily in American social work journals.

Robert T. Golembiewski and Arthur Blumberg (1970) *Sensitivity Training and the Laboratory Approach: Readings about Concepts and Applications.* Itasca, Ill.: F.E. Peacock.

This is an excellent series of thirty-seven readings, on T. Groups and sensitivity training. Of particular interest for social workers are Section I 'What Happens in a T.Group', 'Perspectives and Outcomes', which includes articles on observing, feedback and group development; and Section II 'Who leads a T. Group and How, Perspectives on Trainer and Member Roles'

Section III contains a magnificent article 'How to diagnose Group Problems' by Bradford, Stock and Horwitz quoted at length earlier in this book. There is also much of value about leadership roles and the techniques involved which tend to be so neglected in the social work press.

*Peter B. Smith (1970) *Group Processes* (Modern Psychology Readings). Harmondsworth: Penguin.

This is a collection of very well known contributors in the small group world. Perhaps the following are most significant for social workers:

1. R.T. Golembiewski – 'The Development of the Genus 'Group' on Definitions'
2. D. Cartwright and A. Zander – 'Theoretical Orientations'
5. M.E. Shaw – 'Communication Networks'
13. Fred E. Fielder – 'The Contingency Model: A Theory of Leadership Effectiveness' (A much quoted and very basic work in leadership theory.)
17. Bruce W. Tuckman – 'Developmental Sequence in Small Groups'

There are, of course, other studies which provide interesting material on conformity and on conflict. But as this is a psychology text there is nothing to help the practitioner decide on the practical value of what is offered.

*Henry Walton (1971) *Small Group Psychotherapy* (Science of Behaviour). Harmondsworth: Penguin.

There is no indication in this short paperback of which contributor was responsible for which part. Nevertheless, there is much of interest for the social group work operator here, particularly:

1. 'Technical Procedures in Group Psychotherapy' which outlines the difference between client-centred and group-centred approaches and goes on to indicate very simply group procedures.
2. 'Some Special Characteristics of Groups' which concentrates on the leadership of the 'conductor' which is carried further in:
3. 'The Individual's Relationship in the Group'.

A very readable book bearing in mind that it is analytically and treatment-oriented only, though the emphasis is rather more on the group-centred approach than client-centred.

4) Selected British Material on Practice

These forty-nine articles are readily available from British sources. They have been classified according to setting and purpose so that the wide range of the use of groups should be clear.

A. Crime and Delinquency

Adams, E. and Howlett, J. (1972) 'Working with Clients in the Group Setting or Diversionary Therapy.' *Probation* 18 (2): 54-6.

Ashley, P.D. (1962) 'Groupwork in the Probation Setting.' *Probation* 10 (1) 1.

Ashley, P.D. (1965) 'The Development of a Mixed Group.' *Probation* 11 (3).

Flegg, J. (1972) 'But Probation Officers do run Groups.' *Probation* 18 (2): 56-8.

Freegard, M. (13 Feb.1964) 'Five Girls against Authority.' *New Society*: 18-20.

Gordon, Z. (1971) 'Group Work and Juvenile Offences.' *Probation* 17 (3): 81-4.

Harding, J. (1971) 'Barge Cruising – an Experiment in Group-work.' *Probation* 17 (3): 85-7.

Jones, H. (1965) 'Group Work: Some General Considerations.' In H. Barr (1966) *Probation Service.* H.M.S.O.

Lacka, Y. and Shaw, P. (1966) 'Social Groupwork Training in the General Placement.' *Social Groupwork Information Service Series 1* No. 8.

McCullough, M.K.(21 Feb. 1963) 'Groupwork in Probation.' *New Society* (21): 9-11.

Parsloe, P. (March 1972) 'Why don't Probation Officers run Client Groups?' *Probation* pp. 4-8.

Stanley, A.R. and McCarthy, J. (1965) 'Working with Parents.' In H. Barr (1966) *Probation Service* H.M.S.O.

B. Education and Training

Bilston, W.G. (1968) 'Groupwork training for social workers.' *Social Work.*

Davies, B. (1973) 'The use of T. groups in training social workers.' *Brit. J. of Social Work* 3 (1): 65-7.

Lawrence, G. (1972) 'Some Dangers in Group Training.' *Social Work Today* 3 (4): 10.

Smith, D.E. (1972) Group Supervision: An Experience. *Social Work Today* 3 (8): 13-15.

C. Children

Applin, G.K. and Bamber, R. (1973) 'Group Counselling.' *Social Work Today* 3 (22): 5-9.

Davies, J.W.D. (1965) 'Groupwork and the Deprived Child.' *Case Conference* 12 (7).1

Lavan, A. (1971) 'Simultaneous Groups as a Means of Treatment in a Child Guidance Clinic.' *Social Work Today* 1 (7): 5-11.

D. Adolescents

Gee, H. and Kemp, P. (1969) 'Starting an Adolescent Group.' *Brit. J. of Social Work* 10 (1): 12-16.

E. Parents

Bond, N.A. (13 March 1969) 'A Play Group for Fathers.' *New Society*: 405.

Brown, L.K. and Smith, J. (1972) 'A Group for Mothers.' *Social Work Today* 3 (10): 15-17.

Stockbridge, M.E. (1966) 'The Third Fountain.' *British Journal of Psychiatric Social Work* 8 (3): 43-45.

Vass, F. (1969) 'Application of Group Techniques in Social Work Practice. *Case Conference* 16 (6): 204-211.

F. Foster care

Ball, G. and Bailey, J. (1969) 'A Group of Experienced Foster Parents.' *Case Conference* 15 (12) 1.

Hilson, J.K. and Heaton, D. (1971) 'Common Concerns and Cookies: A Foster Parents' Group in Ontario.' *Social Work Today* 2 (1).

Nyman, J. and Nyman, M. (1971) 'Foster Parents and C.C.Os – An Experiment in Group Work.' *Social Work Today* 2 (1).

G. Adoption

Brown, P.A. (1971) 'Group Meetings for Adopters.' *Social Service News* 1 (5): 7-10.

McWhinnie, A.M. (1968) 'Group Counselling with 78 Adoptive Families.' *Case Conference*

H. Family Group Therapy

Barnes, G.G. (1973) 'Working with the Family Group.' *Social Work Today* 4 (3): 65-70.

Gomersall, J. (1972) 'Family Therapy.' *Drugs and Society* 8 (1): 12-14.

Hopkins, I. (1970) 'Family Group Therapy.' *Social Work Today* 1 (9): 13-15.

Needham, M.A. (1972) 'Working with the Family as a Group.' *Social Work Today* 3 (3): 2-6.

Porter, A. and Tyndale, A. (1971) 'Group Work with Families who Share a Common Problem.' *Social Work Today* 2 (2): 3-6.

Roberts, W.L. (1968) 'Working with a Family Group in a Child Guidance Clinic.' *B.J.P.S.W.* 10 (4): 175-9.

Skynner, A.C.R. (1971) (a) 'Indications for and against conjoint family therapy.' *Social Work Today* 2 (7):3-5.

(b) 'A Group Analytic Approach to Conjoint Family Therapy.' *Social Work Today* 2 (8): 3-11.

(c) 'The Minimum Sufficient Network.' *Social Work Today* 2 (9): 3-7.

I. Health and Medical Care

Brueton, M. (1963) 'An Experiment in Groupwork with Adolescent Skin Patients.' *The Almoner* 15 (12).

Brooks, C. (1961) 'Groupwork with Mothers in a Health Visiting Service.' *B.J.P.S.W.* 6 (2): 62-7.

J. Miscellaneous Groupwork Practice

Family Service Unit (207 Old Marylebone Road, London NW1) 'Groupwork with the Inarticulate.' *F.S.U. Paper No. 1.*

Parsloe, P. (1971) 'What Social Workers say in Groups.' *Brit. J. Social Work* 1 (1): 39-62.

Button, L. (1967) 'Some Experiments in Informal Group Work.' Univ. Coll. Swansea: Group Studies Occasional Paper 2.

Henderson, J. and Leach, A. (1971) 'The Thursday Club: For Adolescents possibly at Risk.' *Social Work Today* 1 (12): 21-4.

Matthews, J. (9 Jan. 1964) 'Social Groupwork in Youth Clubs.' *New Society*: 18-19.

K. Residential Work

Breslin, A. and Sturton, S. (1974) 'Groupwork in a Hostel for the

Mentally Handicapped.' *Social Work Today* 4 (23): 722-6.
Champlin, C.D. (7 Nov. 1963) 'Addict, heal Thyself.' *New Society*: 9-10.
Sugarman, B. (6 June 1968) 'The Phoenix Unit: Alliance against Illness.' *New Society*: 830-32.
Sugarman, B. (13 April 1967) 'Daytop Village: A Drug-cure Cooperative.' *New Society*: 526-29.

L. Theory and Research
Cooper, C.L. (1973) *Group Training for the Helping Professions: the Hampshire Experience in Group Training for Individual and Organisational Development.* Basle, Switz.: S. Karger.
Heap, K. (1964) 'The Scapegoat Role in Youth Clubs.' *Case Conference* pp. 215-21.
(1967) 'The Teaching of Intervention in Social Groupwork: Some Problems and a Point of View.' *Case Conference* 13 (10): 349-56.
(1966) 'Social Groupworker as Central Person.' *Case Conference* 12 (7): 20-29.
Smith, P.B. (25 March 1971) 'Varieties of Group Experience.' *New Society*: 483-85.

5) Other Relevant Articles

Most of this material is American, but presentation has been restricted to those articles which appeared in fairly easily accessible social work journals. The exceptions occur when an article is of considerable importance in the area of the conceptualization of theory which is almost totally ignored in the British Journals.

B. Education and Training
Sales, E. and Navarre, E. (1970) *Individual and Group Supervision in Field Instruction.* University of Michigan: School of Social Work.
This is a research pamphlet which compares student supervision on an individual basis with supervision in groups. The results are well worth reading both for the validation of certain aspects of practice and for a reasonable demonstration of a small research project.

D. Adolescents
Maclennan, B.W. and Felsenfeld, N. (1968) *Group Counselling and Psychotherapy with Adolescents.* N.Y.: Columbia U. Press.
A very informative, succinct paperback which is very readable. It puts a psychotherapeutic approach clearly.

E. Parents
Rose, S.D. (July 1969) 'A Behavioural Approach to the Group Treatment of Parents.' *Social Work* pp. 21-30.

H. Family Group Therapy
Satir, V. (1964) *Conjoint Family Therapy.* Ben Lomond, Calif.: Science and Behaviour Books Inc.
A very useful guide and handbook for those involved in work with families – somewhat irritating presentation.

J. Miscellaneous Groupwork Practice
Hurwitz, J.I. (July 1956) 'Systemising Social Group Work Practice.' *Social Work.* pp. 63-69.
Levine, B. (1965) 'Principles for Developing an Ego-supportive Group Treatment Service.' *Social Service Review* pp. 422-432.
Sturton, Sheila (Summer 1972) 'Developing Groupwork in a Casework Agency.' *British Journal of Social Work* 2: 143-58.

L. Theory and Research
Feldman, R.A. (1969) 'Group Integration, Intense Interpersonal Dislike and Social Groupwork Intervention.' *Social Work* 14 (3): 30-39.
Feldman's work is a clear example of the analysis of practice in order to provide validated guidelines for treatment-oriented groupwork. This is one of the few articles in which techniques are advanced directly from research.

Klein, J.G. (1961) 'Social Group Treatment: Some Selected Dynamics.' In *New Perspectives on Services to Groups.* National Association of Social Workers, pp. 35-48.

Lakin, M. (1972) *Experiential Groups: The Uses of Interpersonal Encounter, Psychotherapy Groups, and Sensitivity Training.* Morristown, N.J.: General Learning Press.

Lang, N.C. (March 1972) 'A Broad-rnage Model of Practice in the

Social Work Group.' *Social Services Review* **46** (1): 76-89.
Lang is suggesting that groups should be set up based almost
exclusively on the assessed ability of the clients to use them,
e.g. those only able to function as individuals need a group
which is leader-centred; those who are able to work for group
goals need a group which is self-directed. Lang posits a
transition stage combining the two extremes.

Levinson, H.M. (1973) 'Use and Misuse of Groups.' *Social Work*
18 (1): 66-73.
A salutary reminder of the wasted potential in a large number
of social work groups because of rigid theoretical approaches.

Papell, C.P. and Rotham, B. (1966) 'Social Groupwork Models:
Possession and Heritage.' *Journal of Education for Social
Work* **2** (2): 66-77.
A clear statement of three main models of practice. This is
a fundamental article for all interested in the conceptualization
of groupwork practice. Two of the models offered here are
examined at length by Sallie A. Churchill in chapter 16 of
Individual Change through Small Groups mentioned earlier.

Shalinsky, W. (1969) 'Group Composition as an Element of
Groupwork Practice.' *Social Service Review* **43** (1): 42-49.
The author uses Schutz's FIRO-B test to demonstrate the link
between the compatibility of the members of a given group
and its subsequent performance. He then postulates that
members of a group can be selected to facilitate group goals,
or if members are not selected with this kind of aim in view,
then goals have to be modified accordingly. Shalinsky backs
up these statements with his own research.

Weiner, H.J. (1964) 'Social Change and Social Groupwork
Practice.' *Social Work* **9** (3): 106-112.
A 'milestone' article which puts forward the thesis that social
work groups should be oriented to social action, i.e. that the
group functioning as an entity should attempt to bring about
social change.

Index

AUTHOR INDEX

SUBJECT INDEX